Organizing Macro-Analysis Seminars:

Study & Action For a New Society

ORGANIZING MACRO—ANALYSIS SEMINARS
A MANUAL

TABLE OF CONTENTS

	Page
I. INTRODUCTION	1
A. What is Macro-analysis	1
B. Why Macro-analysis	1
C. Relation to Social Change	2
D. What is a Macro-analysis Seminar?	3
II. TYPES OF MACRO-ANALYSIS SEMINARS	4
A. The Standard Seminar: 24 & 12 weeks	4
B. Issue-oriented Seminar	4
III. HOW TO RUN A STANDARD MACRO-ANALYSIS SEMINAR	5
A. Introduction	5
B. Overview	5
1. Content	8
2. Resources	8
3. Process	9
4. Individual Responsibilities	9
5. Outline of a typical session	10
C. General Process Roles and Techniques	10
1. Process Roles	11
2. General Process Techniques	13
3. Other Useful Tools and Observations	14
D. Process Ideas for each Major Content Area	14
1. Introductory Sessions	14
2. Analysis Sessions	22
3. Vision Sessions	25
4. Strategy and Action Sessions	25
5. "Where do we go from here?" Sessions	27
E. Variations	27
1. From Micro to Macro	28
2. One Book, All Together	28
3. Reorder the Content	28
4. Change the Content	28
5. Change the Process	29
IV. HOW TO ORGANIZE A SEMINAR	30
A. Introduction	

B. Getting People Together	30
C. Practical Details	30
1. Recruitment	31
2. Preparation for the First Meeting	31
3. Establishing Common Expectations	31
D. Encouragement	31
	32

V. THE MACRO-ANALYSIS MOVEMENT: WHERE IT'S BEEN AND WHERE IT'S GOING

VII. THE PHILADELPHIA MACRO-ANALYSIS COLLECTIVE

        35

VII. THE MACRO-ANALYSIS MOVEMENT: WHAT YOU CAN DO

        37

VIII. MACRO-ANALYSIS AND THE UNIVERSITY

        37

IX. MACRO-ANALYSIS AND SOCIAL ACTION

A. The Need for Action	38
B. Some Examples of Actual Follow-up Activities by Macro-analysis Seminars	38
C. Some Types of Follow-up Activities Your Seminar Might Consider	38
1. Start New Seminars	39
2. Research-Study-Action Projects	39
3. Work With an Organization	39
4. Writing Projects	39
5. Nonviolent Direct Action Projects	39
	39

X. ISSUE-ORIENTED SEMINARS

A. Introduction	40
B. Choosing a Subject	40
C. Setting Up the Seminar Format	40

APPENDIX A: HOW TO DO A "MINI-MACRO"   43

   A. Agenda
   B. Process

APPENDIX B: UNDERLYING PRINCIPLES OF MACRO-ANALYSIS   44

   A. Group Process
   B. Topics
   C. Readings
   D. Action

APPENDIX C: EMPOWERMENT: SOME THEORY AND TOOLS 49
    A. Introduction
    B. Theory
    C. Tools
    D. Resources

APPENDIX D: MORE RESOURCES 55
    A. Community Building
    B. Group Process
    C. Personal Growth (Re-evaluation Counseling)
    D. Direct Action
    E. Researching a Local Community

I. INTRODUCTION

A. WHAT IS MACRO-ANALYSIS?

Macro-analysis is about the "Big Picture." It is a process whereby a group of people can systematically ask some of the most basic questions about the shape and workings of our present world order and their own lives.

The macro-analysis process was developed by a group of us who have been actively involved in the struggle for social justice here in the United States. Beginning with the civil rights movement, and then continuing into the anti-war movement, we discovered along the way that the social problems we were encountering did not exist in isolation — but were profoundly interconnected and were a part of a larger system whose fruits of injustice could be found all over the globe.

Because of our concern to get at the roots of the social and economic problems we faced, we were forced to look deeper and deeper into the workings of our economic system. In order to do that systematically, we organized ourselves into study groups. These study groups were the seeds for the present macro-analysis seminars.

Along the way our seeds have been watered and our ground has been tilled by countless friends, many of whom themselves decided to use the macro-analysis approach. What we present to you in this manual, then, is simply the most recent version of an on-going process of study and dialogue. We hope that you will join us in this dialogue, and contribute whatever insights and suggestions you can to this process of study and action.

B. WHY MACRO-ANALYSIS?

Take the world hunger problem as an example.

Hard on the heels of the energy "crisis," the world has awakened to the shock of a very real food crisis. For those of us who are willing to act for social change, the question is: what can we do to keep half the world from starving?

We are convinced that the solution to this and to other global problems has to begin with a sufficient understanding of the workings of our social and economic system. Otherwise our proposals and our actions may go wide of the mark, *and may even aggravate the problem.*

Here are some "facts on food" that may help to show the complexity of the problem:

■ One key to the food problem is increased food production in the poor countries by the careful application of fertilizer. In lesser developed agricultural regions the use of fertilizer has the effect of substantially raising crop yields. In more developed regions, where agriculture has used fertilizer, the additional yields brought by more fertilization are minimal. Nevertheless, the April 26, 1974 issue of the *Economist* reports that of the additional $4 billion worth of fertilizer that will be produced in 1974, *virtually all of it will go to the agriculturally developed countries.*

■ 90% of the shrimp that is caught off the coast of Mexico is shipped to the United States. If that shrimp were kept in Mexico, a country whose people suffer malnutrition and disease due to protein deficiency, *it would increase the protein intake of each and every Mexican by 25%!*

■ The United States has long patted itself on the back for its massive "Food for Peace" programs. These programs were primarily developed in order to dispose of the agricultural surpluses that had accumulated in America because of our price-support program for our farmers. The bulk of FFP shipments were not given away but loaned on credit to favored developing countries. Thus not only were huge debts created in these countries — debts that today limit their capacity to finance needed projects — but much of the money gained from the sale of the shipments was used to buy arms and munitions from the United States. FFP crop shipments were usually sold on the local market, thus depressing the price for home-grown goods. Local farmers would then switch to more profitable export oriented cash crops like coffee, and this further eroded the recipient nation's capacity for food self-sufficiency.

Perhaps the above examples will give some idea of just how complex a world problem can be. Again and again we have found that the "conventional wisdom" about social and economic problems has proven to be either blind folly or self-serving rationalization. Macro-analysis is designed to go beyond the conventional wisdom so that long-term, meaningful change can result.

C. RELATION TO SOCIAL CHANGE

The most important role of the macro-analysis seminars is to help groups and individuals develop more meaningful *actions for social change.* The goal of concrete action for a more just world society should always be in the minds of seminar members. We see macro-analysis as a *tool* which can be utilized by people in the movement for social change — not as an end in itself.

Seminar members must be careful not to be trapped in what Dr. Martin Luther King called the "paralysis of analysis." That is to say, not spending forever studying the issues and questions and continually putting off moving into action for social change. Our sisters and brothers in the Latin American movement for social change use the word *praxis,* which means action with reflection. Gandhi — one of the world's most notable social activisits — regularly took time for analysis and reflection, a time known by some as "Gandhian Mondays." Macro-analysis seminars are one way in which social activists can spend their Gandhian Mondays together.

Since the macro-analysis seminars began four years ago, a number of social actions have come out of the process of group study. In Seattle, a campaign against local atomic power plants grew directly out of a macro-analysis seminar. In Swarthmore, Pa., a macro-analysis group became so concerned about the "protein swindle" that occurs in world food trade that they organized a special effort to get students to read DIET FOR A SMALL PLANET — a book that aptly discusses the situation.

Perhaps the most spectacular effort to come out of a macroanalysis seminar occurred in 1971, when groups of people in five different port cities blocked the loading of ships destined for the Pakistani Army. Pakistan at the time was attempting to subdue a nationalist revolt in the area that has since become Bangladesh, and its murderous course was being supported with U. S. arms. A macro seminar studying the problem of U. S. support of reactionary regimes abroad was the instigator for this very successful action.

D. WHAT IS A MACRO-ANALYSIS SEMINAR?

The rest of this manual will be devoted to answering this question. Briefly, the macro-analysis seminar is a small-group discussion program organized around a series of proposed readings and utilizing the individual resources of each participant. The seminar outlined in this manual covers seven topic areas: Introduction, Ecology, U. S. Relations with Third World Nations, U. S. Domestic Problems, Visions of a Better Society, Strategies for Social Change, and "Where Do We Go from Here?"
In addition to the extensive bilbiography of readings found in the separate reading list, much of this guide (chapters III, IV, and VII) is devoted to group process suggestions for organizing and conducting this seminar.

Many study and seminar groups have great difficulties with their manner and style of functioning. Many groups which are organized around exciting topics and have attracted interested people seem to get bogged down in poor "process." Some groups lack a shared time discipline and find that they don't cover the material they had wanted to. Some groups are unable to focus on one topic, and wander all over the map. In some groups particularly verbal people may tend to dominate the discussion.

We have worked hard to break these kinds of patterns. The process which we suggest in this manual attempts to be democratic, honest, and encouraging of real sharing. At the same time it allows the group to focus its attention and successfully grapple with the topic at hand. We feel strongly that since equalitarian, open, relationships are a part of our vision of a new society, we must begin now to develop those relationships with each other. The macro process is useful in other settings, including business meetings. We hope to see it spread.

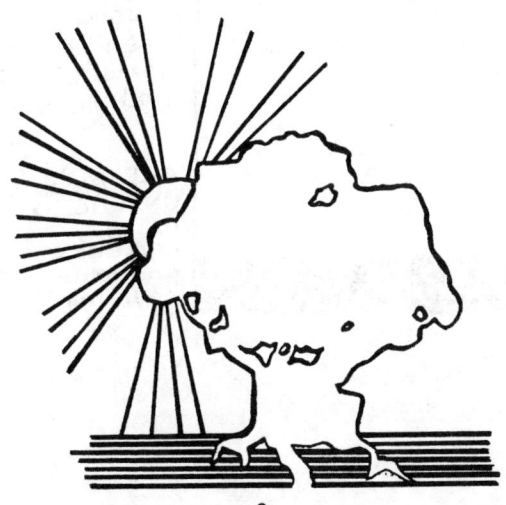

II. TYPES OF MACRO-ANALYSIS SEMINARS

A. STANDARD SEMINAR — 24 AND 12 WEEKS

The standard seminar that has developed over the past five years generally runs for about 24 three-hour sessions. We've found, however, that many groups wanting to do a seminar are unable to give that much time, or have to fit it into one semester at school. To accommodate the needs of such people we have developed a twelve week variety which is essentially a condensed version of the longer seminar. Knowing how superficially even the longer seminar deals with such a broad range of issues, we found it hard to cut it in half, and strongly urge groups to take the time to do the longer one if they possibly can. How to run a standard seminar of the twelve or twenty-four week variety is described in Chapter III.

B. ISSUE ORIENTED SEMINAR

At the conclusion of a seminar, many groups or individuals within them will want to go back to areas of particular concern in greater depth. Although we can't possibly provide seminar outlines for all those areas, some general guidelines and suggestions for setting up such issue oriented seminars are provided in Chapter X.

Capitalism, overconsumption, racism, "democratic-centralism", sexism, pollution....

ARE ALSO UNHEALTHY FOR CHILDREN and other living things.

III. HOW TO RUN A STANDARD MACRO-ANALYSIS SEMINAR

A. INTRODUCTION

This chapter is the "how to do it" part of the manual. We first give a general overview of the content, resources and process for the seminars in Part B, including an outline for a typical session. Part C describes the process roles and some of the techniques that are used in each session, and Part D explains more about each of the major sections (introduction, analysis, visions, strategy, action). In Part E some of the possible variations to the suggested format are discussed.

Remember that these "instructions" are not meant to be followed rigidly. Since a mechanism for change is built in via the evaluation part of each session, it is possible to start with this model and then to experiment with changes, even drastic ones. Folks are encouraged to use this information critically and adjust it when necessary to meet their own group's needs.

B. OVERVIEW

1. Content

The macro-analysis seminar described here is of a general introductory type. We are suggesting two possible lengths, of twenty-four or twelve weeks, with weekly sessions of three hours each. The shorter seminar is basically a condensed version of the 24 week one for use by people who are unable to make a longer time commitment, and the information given below is equally applicable to both.

The seminar's seven topic areas are each subdivided into more specific topics. These subtopics are especially prone to change with the needs of a particular seminar group. The topics and subtopics now are:

(1) INTRODUCTION
    a. Introduction to macro-analysis
    b. Personal introductions, and sharing of expectations and wishes
    c. Exploring and clarifying values and assumptions
    d. Arranging practical details

(2) ECOLOGY
    a. Limits to growth
    b. Food
    c. Population and environment
    d. Environment and pollution
    e. Pollution and technology
    f. Role of energy
    g. Economic and political implications
    h. Alternatives and solutions
    i. Current events and action

(3) U. S. RELATIONS WITH THE THIRD WORLD
    a. Historical and present day perspectives
    b. The loans business
    c. Foreign aid, hunger and the philanthropists
    d. Control and interdependence

    e. The development of underdevelopment
    f. Militarism and the maintenance of oppression
    g. Development: new definitions
(4) UNITED STATES DOMESTIC PROBLEMS
    a. Economics of everyday life
    b. Some social problems
    c. Alienation, consumerism, and irrationality
    d. Historical background
    e. Broad economic perspective
    f. Inequality: poverty and welfare to the rich
    g. Power structure
    h. Role of corporations
    i. Militarism
    j. Current events
    k. Approaches to solutions
    l. Solutions and change movements
    m. Solutions and action
(5) VISIONS
    a. Utopias
    b. Recent visions — theoretical
    c. Recent visions — Gandhi
    d. Recent visions — Marxism and decentralist
    e. Some existing alternatives
    f. Existing alternatives — China
    g. Recent visions — participatory democracy
    h. Some sticky questions
    i. Personal liberation
    j. A woman's vision
    k. To centralize or not to centralize
(6) STRATEGY
    a. Theories of change
    b. The electoral approach to change
    c. Worker's control as a social change strategy
    d. Nonviolent movement approach
    e. Who will make the revolution
    f. Social change history
    g. Strategy for social change — the new left
    h. Strategy — decentralist
    i. Building alternatives
    j. Feminist organizing
    k. Conscientization
    l. Decentralist organizing
    m. Sisterhood is powerful as a social change tool
    n. Personal liberation.

(7) WHERE DO WE GO FROM HERE?

After the introductory sessions, there will be reading material and discussions on each of these subtopics. Time should be allotted in each session to relate the readings to social change actions, including our own, with particular emphasis on trying to develop creative new goals, strategies, and projects for humanitarian social change.

We urge groups to have a general introductory seminar of this type before settling more intensively on any one area, because the causes and solutions to any social problem relate in an important way to all of these areas. Rather than just three or four sessions, many months or even years would be required to adequately cover each one of these areas. But this introductory seminar can acquaint participants with these subjects so that they can get some basic facts, ask some important questions, and begin to see some of the key relationships between these topics, and their implication for social change activities and personal life styles. For example, we cannot adequately work on solving problems of poverty in the U. S. without considering the possible ecological limitation on economic growth; the relationship between U. S. growth and third world poverty, alternative political and economic structures which would optimally solve the problems, and alternative social change methods which might help us achieve our goals.

After completing the general introductory seminar, people are encouraged to go into more depth in an area in which they are interested in doing social change work. Ideas and suggestions for developing such issue-oriented seminars are included in Chapter X .

Each of the major sections of the seminar is briefly described below:
Introduction: We've discovered that it's important, particularly for groups whose members don't know each other well, to spend some time at the beginning sharing basic assumptions, goals, visions for a new society and personal expectations of the seminar. This is also a time for the group to deal with housekeeping details — meeting time and place, finances, duration of the seminar, possible variations, child-care, etc.
Analysis: This section, the major part of the seminar, is planned to provide people with some basic information about the social and economic problems we face with an emphasis on the inter-relationships among problems and their basic causation. Reports and discussion on materials from the three topic areas, ecology, U. S. relations to third world countries, and U. S. domestic problems

are combined with group time to think through their implications for social action and personal change.

Visions of alternatives: Readings about a wide variety of alternative economic social and cultural models are provided as a basis for people to work out their own visions of a good society. With greater clarity about long term goals, thought-about change can be more focused and purposeful.

Strategy: Now that participants have a basic analysis of the problems and a handle on possible solutions, this section deals with different approaches to social change — how to get there from here.

Action: This section provides tools and suggestions to help move a seminar group from study to actual social change work.

2. *Resources*

The following material resources are needed for a seminar:

Macro-analysis manuals: Each participant should have a copy of this manual so that s/he can be familiar with the suggested process and can refer to the readings section in preparing her/his reports.

Reading materials: The books and articles suggested for seminar readings, and how to order them, are listed in the updated reading list.

Recording materials: These consist simply of large crayons (or felt marking pens) and large (about 27" x 34") pieces of paper that can be used for wall charts. *Wall charts* play a central role in the seminars in recording the decisions and thoughts of the group. A tentative agenda for the next week recorded on a wall chart can be a reminder at that week's session of what had been planned. Wall chart sheets are also used to record questions and ideas brainstormed by the group, lists of social change goals and projects, important facts or issues that are raised in reports. These sheets are hung on a wall during each session, can be added to weekly, and serve as a memory bank for the group. Although a blackboard is more ecological and the group might want to use one at times, wall chart sheets have the big advantage of permanence. All the used wall chart sheets are stored throughout the seminar in case they are needed for reference.

Wall chart paper can be scavenged from a friendly print shop or bought in newsprint pads from office or art supply shops. Using both sides of the paper, one seminar usually needs less than sixty sheets. If you cut fiberboard backings for the paper, the wall chart can be put on an easel or a chair for greater visibility.

3. *Process*

With no one person in control, the dynamics of group process become very important, and the skills gained in that area can be as useful as the knowledge people get from the content of the seminar. Techniques of democratic group process have evolved over the years to help groups achieve equal participation and control by all and to assure that groups are not dominated by a few individuals. Ways have also been developed to help overcome superficial manipulation of facts and lack of personal involvement with the subject matter so that we can better integrate our intellectual learning and reflection with our social practices. We have been heavily influenced by Paolo Freire's idea of conscientization in this respect, and recommend special study of his book, PEDAGOGY OF THE OPPRESSED.

Some specific techniques for group process which various seminar groups have developed will be described in this chapter. Since they are different from the familiar teacher-student methods, they may seem awkward and artificial at first. After a few sessions of consciously trying them, however, they become more comfortable, and groups can then decide how much they want to use them.

4. Individual responsibilities

With no leader running a seminar, its success is the responsibility of all the participants and is largely determined by the amount of collective input of time, energy and concern. The more familiar each person is with the alternative processes suggested in this manual and the more responsibility is shared, the less need will there be for a leader or specialist and the more the group will be able to function democratically.

Each participant should be prepared to do the following:
— Read this manual critically at the beginning and use it throughout the seminar
— Be committed to reading a substantial amount of material each week (an average of about 50 pages). This commitment is central to participation in a seminar.
— Assume responsibility for giving a brief report on that reading to the group about every second week (though frequency depends on the size of the group).

— Take on the various group process roles described below on a rotating basis.
— Participate in group discussion without either dominating or allowing others to dominate.

5. Outline for a typical session

A three hour session of a macro seminar will generally include most of the following items and in the order given:

  *1. excitement sharing   10 minutes
  *2. agenda review   2 - 10
  *3. choose assistant facilitator for *next* time   1
   4. brainstorm questions on topic   0 - 20
   5. reports and discussion   20 - 120
  *6. break   5 -15
   7. relate to social change   20 -120

    *8. evaluation of today's session   10 - 15
    *9. plan next session   5 - 20

The items which occur every week will be described in more detail in part C. Items 4, 5, and 7, the bulk of the session will vary at different times in the seminar and according to the needs of the group. Brainstorming questions generally happens only at the beginning of a new topic area. Reports and discussion are often dropped for a session or two at the end of a topic area so that the whole meeting can be focused on relating to social change. Part D, below, describes in more detail the suggested process for each of the major content areas. (You may want to skip over that section in your first reading of this manual.)

C. GENERAL PROCESS ROLES AND TECHNIQUES

1. Process roles

Several specific roles in running a seminar have emerged: convenor, facilitator and assistant facilitator. Recording and keeping time can be done by the assistant facilitator, or they can be separate roles, filled by volunteers each week.

    a. *The convenor* is the person(s) who has gotten the seminar started. That person orders the materials, gets the group together for the first meeting, takes ultimate responsibility for arranging time and place of meetings, and provides the wall chart materials. She or he may also take responsibility for facilitating the first few meetings or getting some experienced facilitators from another seminar group, and may attend between-session planning meetings when needed. If a number of people share these initial responsibilities, there may be no need for a specific convenor.

    b. The *facilitator's* task is to "chair" the meeting, by enabling, or facilitating, the smooth working of the group, and helping it achieve what it wants to achieve. The facilitator should:

— Get the meeting started on time and suggest when it is appropriate to move on (usually based on time limits for agenda items which the group has set for itself)

— Keep reports, discussion and brainstorming sessions within agreed-upon time limits. Remind the group when they have strayed from the agenda, perhaps by asking if they want to return.

— Be sensitive to the feelings of the group; expressions of emotion, types of questions being asked, and general mood may indicate that some variation in process is called for.

— Try to get important but unspoken frustrations, needs, fears, expectations, etc., out in the open so they can be dealt with directly. These "hidden agendas" are often an important source of failure and frustration in groups.

— Help everyone share in the discussion. Be sensitive to shyer people being cut off or intimidated by more extroverted folk. It's often good to ask part way through a meeting if people who haven't participated much have anything they want to say.

— When communication is critical or when hearing seems not to be occurring, ask people to *paraphrase* each other. This means repeating in your own words what you heard the first person say, and then checking with them whether they felt it was an accurate re-statement of what they had said. If not, the person with the "unclear" idea can rephrase it until everyone understands. Telling the person "I think I hear you saying..." will usually obtain the desired result of clarification, and it grates a lot less than "You're not being clear," or "What did you say?"

  c. The *assistant facilitator* helps the facilitator tend to group process by:
— Meeting with the facilitator beforehand to plan that session.
— Assuming some of the responsibilities of running the meeting, such as keeping track of time and recording (see below).
— Being generally aware of how the meeting is running and making suggestions when appropriate to the group.

  d. The *recorder* has the task of writing on the flip charts as it is useful to the group. This may include the agenda, important facts from the reports, brainstormed ideas for action, items from the evaluation. It's sometimes hard to recognize important things to record as they come up, so an open flip chart which everyone can record on as they feel the need might be helpful in addition.

  e. The *timekeeper* helps the group move through the agenda by announcing when agreed-upon times for items are up. It's usually helpful to give people a minute or two of warning, particularly during reports, so that they can use their remaining time well. The timekeeper should be seen as a reminder, not a dictator. When time has run out, the group needs to decide whether to continue that item or move on to the next one.

Rotate roles. The roles of facilitator and assistant facilitator should be filled by as many of the participants as is possible so that the experience and responsibility can be shared. One way to do this is, at every session, to have a new person volunteer to be assistant facilitator for the next session, then move on to become facilitator for the session after that. This gives each person the chance to get a feel for what it's like to have some special concern for group process before taking on full responsibility.

2. General Process Techniques

Group process techniques that are used frequently are described below. They are divided into 1) those which will be used every session, and 2) those which may be used from time to time.

  a. *Excitement Sharing.* This is a good tool for starting each meeting on an "up" note. Sometimes it can be used to draw the group together if people are still milling around and saying hello. The facilitator can call for excitement sharing and when people are seated ask, "What is something good and new that has happened in our lives since we last met?" Each person then has the opportunity to share an event, accomplishment, insight, experience, etc., that was a "plus" during the week. Input should be brief and concise; comments limited.

Some advantages of excitement sharing are: it starts the meeting on a positive note, it develops a more personal tone among the participants, it is enjoyable (and thus may encourage people to arrive on time). Caution: one danger is that excitement sharing could go on for hours. Therefore, don't go beyond an agreed-upon time, say 10 minutes.

b. *Agenda Review.* Near the beginning of every session, the facilitator should present the proposed agenda for the meeting. The agenda can then be reviewed and changed if necessary to accommodate new ideas or different priorities. *The agenda should be recorded on a wall chart or blackboard* in view of the whole group so that everybody can be clear about what they've decided to do.

c. *Choosing the Assistant Facilitator for next week.* At the beginning of the meeting a new person is asked to be an assistant facilitator for the following week. After performing that role, the same person will move on a week later and become the facilitator of the group. This should be a constant process so that everyone will get experience in facilitating the meetings.

d. *Break.* A good break is an essential part of any meeting. A 10 or 15 minute break gives people a chance to stretch, get something to drink, say hello. It is usually hard to keep a time check on breaks, so the group will have to be careful about policing itself.

e. *Evaluation of a session.* It is important to have an evaluation near the end of every meeting. In the evaluation positive and exciting things can be mentioned and affirmed, and perhaps more importantly, participants can identify those items that they didn't particularly like. Often the major focus of the evaluation is on the process — how people interacted, how the ground rules held up, etc. — and this is a good time for "brainstorming" new process ideas.

During the evaluation, the group should brainstorm and/or discuss:
- What was good about the meeting.
- What was bad about the meeting (with constructive suggestions).
- Brief discussion and the selection of the most promising proposals for use in later meetings. (Often the details don't need to be worked out by the group, but can be refined by the facilitator and the assistant facilitator in their planning meeting.)

Each item above should probably be handled separately. If reactions, suggestions, and discussion are all being handled at the same time, it will be hard to stay within time limits and difficult to get everyone's input.

f. *Planning and Preparation for Next Meeting.* Set the agenda for next meeting. (What ground to cover and how to organize your time.)

Individuals should assume responsibility for reporting on specific readings at the next session. This selection process will take little time if the materials are grouped according to report numbers before the session begins.

The facilitator, assistant facilitator, perhaps the convenor, and other interested participants should meet between sessions when it is necessary to detail and develop plans for the next meeting.

3. *Other Useful Tools and Observations*

a. *Think and Listen.* This technique is sometimes very helpful when the group wants to hear in some depth what each individual thinks about a particular topic or question. In a "think and listen" session each participant is given a set amount of time to share their thoughts while the rest of the group listens attentively without comment or question. People should be encouraged to "think out loud" and needn't be apologetic if their comments aren't organized in precise categories and steps. Time limits should be strictly observed. It is usually helpful to inform the speaker when s/he has one more minute remaining, so that s/he can wind up her/his thoughts. If time is a problem, the group can split into "think and listen pairs" and then bring important points back to the whole group.

b. *Brainstorming.* Brainstorming is a process that is used to gather a large number of creative ideas or questions on a given subject from a group in a relatively short period of time. In brainstorming, the group picks a topic or question and then opens the floor for people to toss in ideas. Participants are encouraged to throw in ideas, no matter how wild or impractical they may seem. Each idea is recorded on a wall chart or blackboard in front of the group. *There is no discussion and no evaluation of the ideas during this part of the exercise.*

Once a lengthy list of ideas has been collected, the group can then go back and sift out the proposals that seem the most promising. A good brainstorming session rarely needs to go longer than 20 minutes and often can be done in less time. In groups larger than six it is often helpful to expand participation by limiting each person to one or two brainstormed ideas before everyone else has contributed.

Brainstorming can be used for a variety of situations. It can be helpful in suggesting new process arrangements during an evaluation session. It can be a good way to generate action proposals for a project idea (for example, What can we do to end US exploitation and military involvement in Brazil?) It can be used to develop questions for the evening's discussion (for example, What questions do we want to raise about ecology?).

c. *Time Limits.* It is usually frustrating, and essentially anti-democratic, when a group is lax about the time it has allocated to various portions of the agenda. (The agenda can, of course, be changed, but this should only be with the consensus of the group.) There will be tendencies in every group to go beyond the time limits, especially when the subject is of great interest. This often happens in report-giving. The time limits we suggest are based on the experience of seeking a balance between too little time for substantive reports and giving so much time that people lose interest and other areas go unreported. We suggest a maximum of 10 minutes for a report on an entire book and 5 minutes for the usual 50 pages of reading.

There may well be particular reports of sufficient interest to the group that it makes a conscious decision to suspend the "rules" and extend the time. The group can decide in advance whether it wants to allow proposals for extension at the end of each report or after all have been given.

Time limits are important to watch for in every item of the agenda: breaks, excitement-sharing, evaluation, etc. It is very helpful to ask one person to keep track of time during each section of the agenda. This role can be rotated during the meeting, or filled for the entire session by one person, such as the assistant facilitator.

d. *Web Chart.* This visual process enables a group to trace the root causes or effects of any specific concrete social condition. It quite literally results in a "big picture," locating the issue of concern in the center of a web of forces directly related to it. It facilitates a group analysis of a problem and, by indicating "handles" on the problem, can be of considerable value also in helping the group plan a strategy.

The group starts by writing the issue of concern in the center of a blackboard or wall chart, such as "negative consequences of heavy American reliance on the automobile" or "the inadequacy of health care in our town." Group members then suggest what they feel are important *causes* or *consequences* of the problem. (The group should decide in advance to concentrate *just* on consequences *or* causes; don't mix them.) As group members suggest various items, they are placed on the board around the central concern and connecting lines are drawn from each item to the central problem. When the group is satisfied that major direct causes have been identified, they then concentrate on what they feel are the causes of those major direct causes, which in turn are causing the central problem. As numerous second and third and even fourth-level causes are added, the diagram assumes the appearance of a web. *Note:* it is very important to make the central issue on which you concentrate a *very concrete* one; if it is too vague you will soon become lost in questions of what various terms "really" mean. The entire procedure can take from half an hour to an hour.

D. PROCESS IDEAS FOR EACH MAJOR CONTENT AREA

1. Introductory Sessions

The 24 week seminar begins with three introductory sessions. The experience of previous seminars has been that this time at the beginning lays the ground for a smoothly functioning group throughout the seminar. The purposes of these three weeks include:

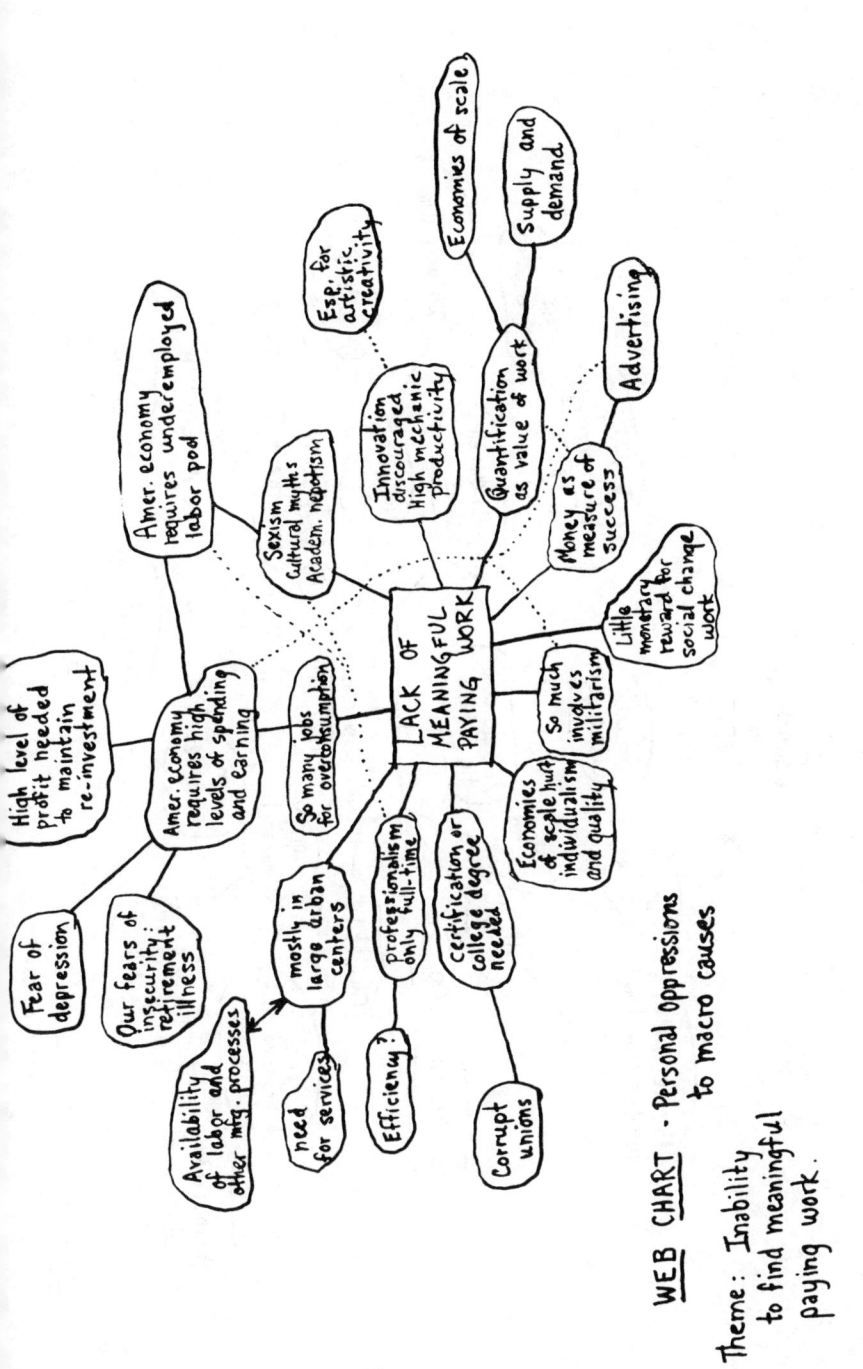

WEB CHART - Personal oppressions to macro causes

Theme: Inability to find meaningful paying work.

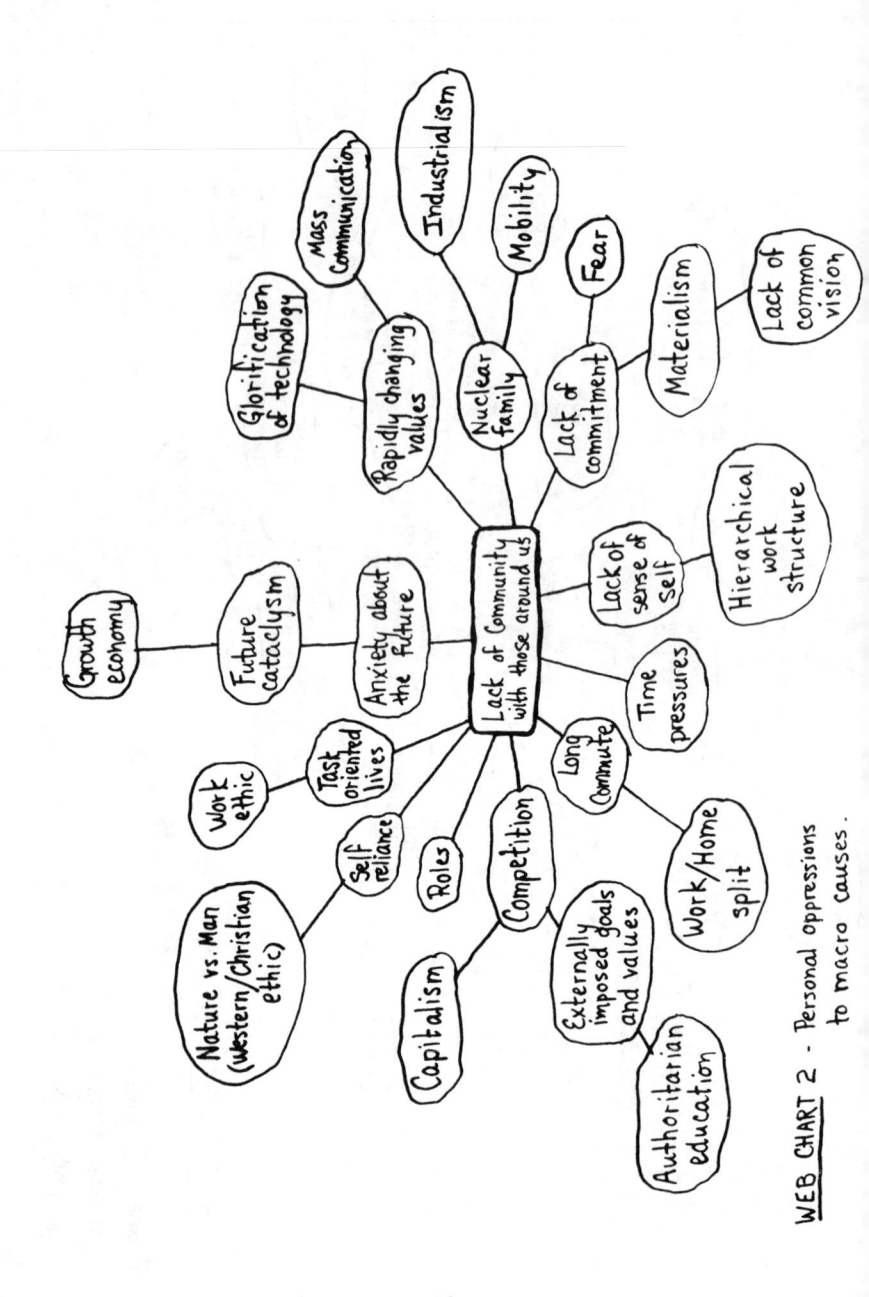

WEB CHART 2 - Personal oppressions to macro causes.

- Personal introductions and getting to know each other
- Building group trust
- Deciding on mechanics of the seminar such as time, place, etc.
- Sharing expectations for the seminar and hopes for what might come out of it.
- Exploring personal values
- Beginning to think about the society we live in, how it affects us, and how we would like to see it changed.

To this end we suggest the following possible agendas for the first three sessions:

Week 1	minutes
Excitement sharing	5
Agenda review	5
Personal Introductions	up to 60
Introduction to macro-analysis	15
Break	10
Share expectations and wishes for the seminar	15
Initial business	up to 30
Brainstorm visions for a new society	10
Distribute macro-analysis manuals	5
Evaluation	5
Week 2	
Excitement sharing	5
Agenda review	5
Discussion and questions on macro-analysis manual	15
Business (if necessary)	up to 30
Values clarification exercise	30
Break	10
Personal oppression to macro forces web chart	60
Evaluation	10
Week 3	
Excitement sharing	5
Agenda review	5
Business (if necessary)	up to 30
Values clarification exercise	50
Break	10
Personal liberation to macro forces web chart or vision gallery	60
Brainstorm questions on ecology	10
Evaluation	10
Distribute ecology readings	5

Description of process exercises for the introductory sessions
  a. *Personal introductions*

The extensiveness of personal introductions will depend on how well members of the group already know each other, but even groups in which members know each other are encouraged to spend some time on this. Groups can

choose from the following suggestions of things to be shared by participants, or others they may think of, according to their needs:
1. Name
2. Where you're from
3. How you heard about macro-analysis
4. Why you're interested in a macro-analysis seminar
5. What the basis for your concern with social change is
6. What effect your economic/social/cultural background has had on your political viewpoint.
7. *One thing* you have done well in social change, and one thing you would like to be able to do better.
8. *One thing* you would like to be doing in social action; what is preventing you from doing it; and what you can do about that.
9. Share one or two significant consciousness-raising experiences in your life.

Many introductions lend themselves to being done in *pairs,* with each person turning to her/his neighbor (or to someone s/he doesn't know very well) and introducing him/herself to the other in about three minutes. Then the other person does the same. This "reversal of roles" occurs when the facilitator calls out (loudly!) for everyone to change. Then people introduce their partners to the group as a whole. The content of what people say to each other in the pairs may range over many themes, so individuals should not be expected to be able to remember everything to re-tell to the group.

It is *not* a good idea to ask people simply to tell what social change work they have done, since that often produces a situation where a few people in the group talk at length about their experience while others feel inadequate because they have had less experience. No matter what introductory process is used, each person's comments should be fairly brief and each person should have approximately equal time to share with the group. This basic principle is important to keep in mind throughout the seminar.

b. *Introduction to macro-analysis*

The person convening the seminar may want to take 5 or 10 minutes to give some background information on macro-analysis. This should include definition, historical background, content, process, and relationship to social action, and should be kept brief. The introduction to this manual provides much of this information. A few minutes at the end might be allotted for such questions or discussion as are essential in order to proceed but this should be kept to a minimum since the best way to understand macro-analysis is to do it.

c. *Brainstorming expectations and wishes for the seminar*

A quick brainstorm, with ideas recorded so the group can refer to it later is a good way of checking out whether people's expectations are realistic and whether the seminar is meeting them. Either a brainstorm or a "think and listen" session might be focused by asking people to tell the group (1) ways in which they see themselves using what they will learn from the seminar, or (2) a major hope or goal they have for the seminar. If people have unrealistic or contradictory expectations, this should be made clear and dealt with at this time.

d. *Business*

Groups will vary widely on exactly what items need to be covered and the amount of time involved, so our time estimates are approximate. Possible items are time, length, and place of meetings, length of seminar and commitment to attend regularly, financing cost of reading materials, choosing a librarian to keep reading materials in order, and child care if appropriate. Business items can easily expand to fill the time available, so they should be dealt with efficiently so that other items are not neglected. If it appears that business will take significantly longer than the allotted time, it should be postponed to the next week, perhaps asking a small group to come up with a specific proposal on the item(s) in question to be presented at the next meeting.

e. *Reading and discussion of macro-analysis manual*

The creation of democratic group process, in which everyone participates equally and takes equal responsibility for the success of the seminar, requires that everyone in the group read and be familiar with this manual. Ideally this should be done before the first meeting. If this is not possible, time for reading and discussing the manual should be built into the introductory period in such a way as to permit any clarification or group decision-making needed before the group moves into the analysis sessions of the seminar.

f. *Values Clarification Exercises*

A good exercise that several groups have used to help participants define what aspects of life (values, freedoms, possessions, etc.) are most important to them involves listing in three categories 1) things we would give up under no circumstances, 2) things we would give up for a better society, and 3) things we'd be willing to share. It might be good to announce this exercise the week before so that people can think through their own ideas ahead of time. Then during the meeting the whole group or two smaller groups can combine their ideas and list them on a wall chart. This exercise can also be done during the ecology section.

Removing barriers to action: Often it is much easier to take a stand than to act on it. This exercise is designed to help identify and remove barriers to action. Each person should write at the top of a piece of paper an action s/he would like to take but is having difficulty taking. Each person then draws a line lengthwise down the middle of the paper. On the right hand side, list all the perceived or real barriers, both within and outside yourself, which seem to be keeping you from acting. On the left hand side of the paper, list steps you could take which might help reduce or remove each of the barriers. Finally, on the back of the paper, develop a plan of action for actually removing the barriers. The task may be done individually or in small groups with each of the group members taking turns having the focus and receiving help from the group.

Getting started: Many of us have grandiose plans which we find difficult to put into action. This exercise encourages people to move toward action as well as to ask the question, "Am I really doing what I want to do with my life?" Each person should prepare a sheet of paper with three columns headed "What I want to do," "Date," "First steps." Each person should list up to five things s/he wants to do and assign logical realistic dates to each item. Then list the first steps to be taken in getting started. Then divide into small groups with each person getting a turn as focus person. The focus person discusses what s/he hopes to do and how s/he intends to get started. Other group members give feedback and additional suggestions for getting started.

The previous two exercises are adapted from the book VALUES CLARIFICATION, A HANDBOOK OF PRACTICAL STRATEGIES FOR TEACHERS AND STUDENTS by Simon, Howe and Kirschenbaum. This book contains many exercises which interested groups could adapt for use in the seminar.

g. *Personal oppressions to macro forces web chart*

Most of us feel oppressed by certain elements in the society around us, but often we are not clear about the connections between our personal feelings of oppression and societal forces. This exercise is designed to help make these connections clearer.

1. Participants begin by thinking for 5 - 10 minutes about what aspects of their lives really hurt. These may vary widely: oppression of housework, frustration on a job, traffic jams, the hurt at seeing people killed far away. Each person picks the three most important oppressions to report to the group, and these are listed on a wall chart or blackboard.
2. The group then reviews the list and attempts *quickly* to pick out common themes of the problems, perhaps combining a number of specific problems under one general category. While no single theme is likely to be mentioned by everyone, the group should be able to agree on the importance of several themes. One item is then selected which everyone can identify with at least to some extent. This, too, should be done quickly, recognizing that it probably will not be possible to select something which everyone will feel strongly about.
3. The item chosen is then recorded in the middle of a large wall chart (several taped together are often useful) or blackboard. The group then proceeds to construct a web chart as described in section C of this chapter.
4. Several ways of bringing this exercise to a useful finish have been tried, as follows:
    a) When the web chart is complete, group members should list items toward the edge of the web which are most important to them.

The group selects from that list an item which might be changed by social action, and then each person says what s/he wishes could be true about that situation. The group then selects one of the wishes and carries out the "problem-solution-action" exercise described on page 23.
   b) A brainstorm and discussion on action projects to attack the causes of the central oppression is held.
   c) The group brainstorms questions for further research and analysis.
5. Since the overall process takes at least an hour, it is unlikely that more than one theme can be followed through in a single meeting of a group.

   h. *Personal liberations web chart*
   This exercise, like the one described previously, uses the web chart but focuses on personal liberations, as follows:
   1. Group members think briefly about conditions they personally would like to have in a good society, e.g., good mass transit, work for income no more than two days a week, or close sharing with neighbors.
   2. Each person then shares these with the group, and the group brainstorms additional personal liberations for a few minutes. All items mentioned are listed on a wall chart.
   3. After one item has been chosen to pursue further, people build a web chart around it by thinking of what would be needed to bring this liberation to exist in society, and then what would be needed for those conditions to exist. The outside ring eventually will consist of large-scale social forces necessary for the emergence of the original personal liberation in the center.
   4. If the exercise is done for several personal liberations (perhaps by subgroups working simultaneously), all the macro forces for all the web charts can be put on a wall chart entitled "visionary macro forces."

   i. *vision gallery*
   This is an effective technique for helping people to think of positive, achievable aspects of a good society.
   The group divides into small groups of 3 - 5 people each. Each person takes 15 - 20 minutes to write down major features of a really good society which s/he would like to see. Assume there are no constraints of money, political power, etc. This individual thinking can be done from several different perspectives, and it is generally best if all members of the subgroup agree approximately what perspective they would like to adopt. Possible perspectives include: a description of a major function in such a society, e.g., health care, education, transportation; a description of the kind of community one would like to live in; what kind of work people would do, and where they would live; or a description of "a day in my life" in a good society. When these descriptions are completed, each person shares his or her ideas with the rest of the small group. Then the group combines the best points of all its ideas and records them on a wall chart. This may take the form of a picture, a graph, or a list of items. When the small groups are finished, they come together and hang their papers side by side on a wall in a gallery of visions of a new society. Spokespeople for each small group explain the main points of their vision. The procedure can take from 45 minutes to 1½ hours from start to finish depending on the group's wishes.

Groups should regard these suggestions for the first three weeks as flexible and adapt them to their own particular needs in order to be ready to move on to the analysis section of the seminar.

2. Analysis Sessions

a. Reports on readings, and discussion

Most of the information in the seminar is acquired by a process of reports and discussion. Participants share information and insights from their readings through a short verbal report at the end of which five or ten minutes are given to clarifying questions and group discussion. Then another report can be given. Usually there will be somebody who feels that his or her report follows logically on that discussion, or the group can follow the order suggested in the readings section of this manual. The "report and discussion" part of the agenda, therefore, is basically a long discussion in which every ten or fifteen minutes there is about five minutes of input in the form of a report on that general subject matter. This format has been developed to share out the responsibility for providing factual information while giving lots of space for active group participation. Having prepared reports interspersed through the discussion and time limits helps people to focus and keep from getting sidetracked too much, and it adds a sense of accomplishment and progress to the meeting. The five minutes for reports and ten for discussion are suggested times; each group will want to work out for itself what feels most comfortable depending on time constraints and amounts of information to be covered. Our experience is, however, that whatever time limits are decided upon, people should be disciplined in keeping to them.

How to give a report:
- Start by referring to the report number so that others can scan the titles.
- It's easy to get frustrated by the prospect of condensing 40 or 50 pages of information into a five minute report and the temptation is often to talk twice as fast as usual in order to get everything in. Don't. We can't digest it that quickly. Instead of trying to summarize, pick out the two or three most important points or insights that you got from the readings and explain them. While five minutes is very short for a rambling discourse, a well-organized report can say a great deal. (Think of the impact of a good one-minute TV advertisement.)
- Don't get trapped by paralysis of analysis. As you go into the reading, think about what problems are being identified, what solutions are being suggested, and what the implications are for personal change and social action. Spend some time in your report on the latter — what new goals and/or projects might social change groups adopt according to the reading? The recorder should write these ideas on permanent wall chart sheets as reports are given and during group discussion. Experiment with the procedures suggested for this in the next section.
- Criticize the reading. Are important points backed up by hard reliable data? Were the ideas and inferences of the authors logical?
- Prepare visual aids to go along with the report if appropriate. (Statistics, for instance, are often easier to see than to hear.)

— Put time into preparation of the report. This is helpful not only to make a clearer presentation to others but also to consolidate the learning that you have done.

Role of the facilitator in reports and discussion: The facilitator should keep the reports to the agreed-upon time. This stimulates the reporter to think and select out the best ideas rather than rehashing the readings, and allows time for full group discussion of the issues. If the report is not finished then, any key points remaining might be mentioned during the discussion period.

b. *Relating to social change*

The main purpose of macro-analysis seminars is to improve our social change activities. Consequently, many group processes have been developed to help people create better social change activities and personal lifestyle changes. If groups don't act to help resolve the problems they talk about, they suffer from feelings of powerlessness and become frustrated and inactive. It is important, therefore, that groups use some or all of the following methods often, and invent new ones as well.

•*Every verbal report.* Every time a report is given, the last minute might be devoted to social change implications: new goals, criticism of old goals and present programs, and specific projects we could do. If the allotted time period is about up and the reporter hasn't focused on social change implications, the facilitator can remind that person to do so, or suggest that an extra minute be taken at the end for that specific purpose.

•*Problem-Solution-Action.* We suggest that this exercise be used frequently in the 20-minute social change time near the end of each meeting on ecology, Third World and domestic analysis sections. It helps groups to rapidly gather together much assorted analysis information by listing the problems discussed, possible solutions to them and specific actions people can take to help achieve the solutions. Focusing on actions helps prevent people from becoming depressed and bogged down in too much disheartening analysis.

    1) The recorder makes three columns on *wall charts* and heads them "problems," "solutions or visions" and "social actions: projects or personal lifestyle changes."

    2) For 2 minutes the group *brainstorms the problems* which were discussed in that session and the recorder rapidly writes them in the "problems" column of the wall chart. Add another minute if the group is going strong and wants more time.

3) For 2 minutes the group *brainstorms solutions* to the problems listed in the first column and the recorder rapidly writes the solutions in the second column. Add another minute if needed.

4) For 2 minutes the group *brainstorms projects* that groups could adopt and *lifestyle changes* individuals might take to achieve the solutions in column two. Add another minute or two if needed.

5) *How to do a specific project.* The facilitator asks the group quickly to choose one of the projects or lifestyle changes that were brainstormed. The facilitator then asks, "How could we achieve that?" and the group brainstorms its answers while the recorder writes them on a new wall chart. The list should be positive ideas without criticisms. When the group feels that the list is long enough, the facilitator again asks the group to pick an item from this newly brainstormed list and repeats the question, "How could we accomplish this?" This cycle of selecting a project idea and brainstorming how it could be accomplished is repeated 3 or 4 times until the projects and lifestyle changes become specific, clear and achievable. This whole procedure takes from 30 to 45 minutes, but can be shortened and done in 20 minutes.

■ *Problem-Solution-Project (An alternative method).* Each session before the first report begins, the recorder makes 3 columns on the wall chart, headed "problems," "solutions" and "projects." Then, as each report is given, and during discussion, the recorder extracts any problems, solutions or projects mentioned, and writes them in the appropriate column. This helps focus the discussion more on social change, helps the group produce more useful and practical ideas, and is a good memory device. All the past "action" wall charts could be brought out and hung up each week, and especially during the special sessions on social change.

■ *Personal Oppressions to Macro Forces — Web Chart.* See the description in the previous section.

■ *Critical Analysis of Existing Programs and Lifestyles:* things we're doing and/or that we know others are doing. This could lead into dialogue with these groups.

■ *Developing a list of opposing goals or directions for social action and debate them.* For example, economic growth vs. de-development, capitalism vs. socialism, increasing U. S. foreign aid vs. stopping it, universal vs. selective approach to alleviating American poverty.

■ *Strategy Exercise.* After selecting a well-defined social change goal, e.g., "converting Honeywell Corporation to socially valuable production in 10 years," the seminar group splits into two groups, one of which plays the role of nonviolent direct action advocates while the other plays the role of liberals who advocate always working within established structures to bring about change. Each team is given a separate working place and approximately half an hour in which to produce a program for attaining the specific social change goal. (Each team works toward the same goal.) The programs should specify what they will have accomplished at the end of year one, year two, etc. At the end of the time period, both groups come back together and share their strategies with each other. This sometimes develops into an informal debate and sheds light on the often unnoticed interdependence of such groups.

■ *Mini-actions.* Although many of the social actions that we know about have been big affairs such as marches on Washington, there are many important, smaller activities which a seminar group can do without too much time and effort. Perhaps a seminar would want to do some kind of mini-action once a month: writing a leaflet on a chosen issue and giving it out at some appropriate place or helping a local group by joining their demonstration.

■ *Social Problem to Macro Forces — Web Chart.* This is similar to the personal oppressions web chart above, but instead of picking a personal problem to start with, use a social problem which the group is concerned about.

3. Vision Sessions
    a. *Variations on Vision Gallery.* 1) What might this community look like ten years from now, ideally? 2) What would a day in my life look like in this community? In an ideal society? 3) What kind of factory would I like to work in? 4) What would the U. S. look like?
    b. *Vision Scenario Writing.* Participants write a description answering the question, "What would a good society/world/town/personal life look like in 10 years if the most optimistic changes (though kept within realistic bounds) occurred?" These probably should be written at home between sessions because they would take too much time. The scenario can be written as if it is a newspaper story in 1985 describing conditions as they exist then compared to 1975.
    c. *Brainstorm Characteristics of a Good Society.* Hang wall charts with five columns marked "Economic," "Political," "Social," "Personal" and "Other." The group successively brainstorms characteristics of a good society for each of the topics. Then the facilitator tries to find out which characteristics are agreed to by the whole group and which aren't. For those that don't get agreement, people with opposing views could briefly tell their reasons and each characteristic is again tested for consensus to see if it is on or off the list of agreed-upon visionary characteristics.
    d. *Personal Liberations to Vision Macro Forces — Web Chart.* See the description of this technique in the previous section.
    e. *Visionary Personal Preferences.* See the description under "Values Clarification Exercises" in the previous section.
    f. *Think and Listen.* The group is given silent time (5 minutes) as each person thinks of aspects of a good society which are important to him/her. Then everyone takes 3 minutes to tell his/her key vision ideas to the whole group. A recorder could list unrepetitive ideas on a wall chart. This format can also be used at other times when it is important to get everyone's thoughtful opinion such as difficult situations requiring a group decision.

4. Process Ideas for Strategy-Action Sessions. Most of the processes listed for use in the analysis section above can also be used here. Additional ones are described below:
    a. *Force Field Analysis.* This tool is very useful in helping a group organize information about an up-coming decision or dilemma in such a way as to clarify possible solutions and their implications. If the group knows it would prefer a particular solution, force field analysis can help to specify the obstacles which must be overcome, and combined with other tools, to suggest how much and what kind of effort may be required to overcome them.

A frequent use of the tool is to help a group answer the question, "Should we carry out this possible direct action campaign or not?" Or, in other words, "Is the campaign likely to be successful?" Assuming that the group has a working definition of what success means to it, it proceeds with the analysis by asking, "What are the forces and factors which will contribute to the failure of this project, and what forces will contribute to its success?" This results in 2 lists of forces, one positive and one negative. The beginning of such lists might look like this:

Should we carry out this campaign or not?

Forces contributing to its success (+)	Forces contributing to its failure (−)
1. The issue is of real concern to people in a wide spectrum of local groups.	1. The police department is extremely repressive and paranoid.
2. We have good contacts with sympathetic people in the media.	2. Local action groups aren't accustomed to really working with one another.

Looking at the 2 lists on a blackboard or wall chart, the group judges their relative weight on a mental seesaw to determine which set of forces is heavier. This involves not merely noting which list is longer, but generally deciding which set of factors the group feels carries the most total force. If the negatives outweigh the positives, the group tries to weaken or remove some of the negatives and to add more positive factors. E.g., "We could hold a weekend training session which would be planned and participated in by all local action groups that would be involved, to determine how well we all can really work together." Trying to change the overall balance may require an interim period of information-gathering before a final decision is reached. If the seesaw can be tipped in favor of the success of the project, the group is ready to proceed.

Much of the value of the force field analysis is in the shared thinking through of the factors to be put on the lists. The two lists, when completed and placed side-by-side, offer a wholistic perspective to an extent not often enough produced by a group considering a direct action campaign. It can be used for many purposes, of course: deciding whether or not to publish a pamphlet, start a food co-op, take a new member into a community, or determine whether a particular type of campaign will be useful in dismantling the military-industrial-complex.

 b. *What Other Groups Are Doing.* Contact various social change organizations: get their literature and talk with members. See the literature and groups suggested in Chapter IV, Section C, "How to Keep Your Seminar Updated." Particularly look for groups mentioned in the books CREATING THE FUTURE: A GUIDE TO LIVING AND WORKING FOR SOCIAL CHANGE and THE ORGANIZER'S MANUAL.

 c. *See Other Sections of this Manual for Ideas.* See especially Chapter VII, "The Macro-analysis Movement — What You Can Do.. and Chapter IX "Macro-analysis and Social Action."

5. *Process Ideas for "Where Do We Go From Here?"*
It is extremely important for groups to spend at least one session at the end of their seminar considering their next steps. The following procedures should help.
   a. *Vision-Action Crystal Ball.* This exercise helps groups to relate future visions to the development of social actions today.

      1) Individually or in small groups *predict* how the world, nation and your own life might look ten years from now if present trends continue.

      2) Share these briefly with the whole group.

      3) Individually or in small groups write a description of your vision of the world, nation, local community or your personal life ten years from now if maximum success for positive change happens (be *very* optimistic but not impossibly unrealistic). It might be written as if it is a newspaper article at that time describing conditions.

      4) Then write a scenario of events that lead up to the good society. What caused the changes? Be specific as possible. Emphasis here is on the causes that brought about the good society, not so much of a description of the good society itself. Try to make it believable.

      5) What role did groups you're involved with play? What did you do? What did you do in the first year (i.e., the next year from today)?

      (This exercise can also be used for specific issues and shorter time periods such as the energy crisis over the next 5 years or U. S. support of dictatorships over the next 3 years or nuclear energy.)

   b. *Personal Sharing.* In small groups of 2 or 3 people each, individuals share their hopes, plans, goals, for their own social change activities in the next 12 months. Do you hope the people in this macro-analysis seminar continue as a group? If so, what do you hope the group does next? If you would like to spend more time on social change, what barriers are in your way? What are some ways you might overcome these barriers? Small groups report to the whole group.

   c. *Next Steps for the Group.* While individuals are reporting their personal goals to the whole group (during the personal sharing exercise above), the recorder writes these on a wall chart. On another chart the recorder writes individuals' ideas of what the group as a whole might do. After individuals give their reports, the group focuses on the future of the macro group.

Even if the group chooses not to become an action group, it might decide to stay together to support individuals' actions in other groups they belong to or to provide a forum for ongoing analysis of current events and individuals' actions. Ideally the group should stay together either until it makes plans for action or until individuals feel clear about their personal directions.

E. VARIATIONS

The whole section above on how a macro-analysis seminar runs is presented not as a confining set of rules and regulations but as a description of what seems to work well and as a structure that many different groups can use, adapting and building on it to fit their own needs. Some of the many possible variations are described below.

    a. *From micro to macro:* A seminar group already engaged in, or just beginning, a common social change project, may prefer to begin with readings directly related to that project. Care should be taken to select readings which cover a variety of points of view and put the problem in the context of the big picture. For example, a group working to convert General Electric from military to peaceful, useful work while demanding more worker control could start with a session or two using readings such as:

- G. E. annual report and other public relations literature
- government documents, especially congressional hearings, about G. E.'s military contracts and labor relations.
- literature from The G. E. Project, 48 Inman St., Cambridge, MA 02139
- union literature.

Likewise, a group could begin with a special interest focus such as sexism, criminal justice, welfare rights, or stopping nuclear power plants. After a few sessions on this special interest, the group could proceed with the seminar as outlined in this manual, to discover how that problem is connected with others and fits into a larger analysis.

    2. *One book, all together:* An advantage of having everybody read the same material is that a foundation of common knowledge is provided which helps people move forward in their learning as a group. People can take responsibility for reporting on different parts of the book so that the session can be done using the normal macro-analysis process. A good book to read is REVOLUTION: A QUAKER PRESCRIPTION FOR A SICK SOCIETY (new title: MOVING TOWARD A NEW SOCIETY), which was written by people in one of the first macro-analysis seminars as a way of communicating a summary of what they had learned. Participants might want to work out a combination of common readings and separate reports which bring in a variety of points of view.

    3. *Reorder the content:* Some groups prefer to do the ecology section after the section on U. S. relations with the Third World. We put ecology first because there's some logic in looking at the physical and technological limitations to human existence before looking at political and economic problems; these limitations are the widest and most final constraints on possible solutions to problems to be kept in mind. Other groups might want to spend more time building visions before getting into the analysis section.

    4. *Change the content:* We've tried to provide readings that cover a broad range of material, offer a variety of points of view and come in some logical order, and we'd suggest major changes only after thoughtful consideration. We urge you, however, to bring in new materials such as the following:

- Readings that more adequately deal with the particular concerns of the group. Hopefully these concerns are raised in brainstorming sessions at the beginning of each topic area.
- Current newspaper and magazine articles that update existing reports.
- Literature from local social change groups, particularly if it relates a local problem to macro phenomena and calls for action.

— Literature such as statements of purpose of social change organizations in which members of the seminar are interested.

See Chapter IV for more ideas on adding new and relevant readings. BEWARE: There is a danger in adding so much new material that the group gets bogged down in the middle and never gets through to the end of the seminar which is the most exciting part. You might want to go once through the seminar, then return to special interest material in more depth. (See Chapter X on issue oriented seminars.)

5. Change the process: For a group to keep functioning in an egalitarian and efficient way, some things seem vital: sharing leadership, equalizing participation, having everyone understanding and being comfortable with what's going on. Once you've gotten a feel for the basic processes, however, there's lots of opportunity for modification and creativity — good and new process ideas are emerging all the time. Groups in the past have tried typing up and duplicating reports for distribution, having potluck dinners before seminar meetings, spending Saturdays playing and getting to know each other, scrapping facilitation and time-keeping for a session to see how it feels, having individuals choose the time limits for their own reports, and dividing up into groups of three or four for social change discussion.

An example of a valuable experiment in changed process is the procedure used by a seminar in Kalamazoo, Michigan. Their experience may be useful to other groups. In the first hour or hour and a half normally reserved for reports and discussion they substituted an open discussion focused on a question that they chose the previous week. The question would be general enough so that most of the readings for that session would be relevant to it. If, at the end of the discussion time one or more persons felt that they had not had a chance to contribute from their reading, they would then give a short report. This style worked in the Kalamazoo group because the members accepted a self discipline that allowed equal participation. In groups where a few people tend to dominate discussion, the standard format should be more helpful.

IV. HOW TO ORGANIZE A SEMINAR

A. INTRODUCTION

This chapter is designed mainly for people who are definitely interested in macro-analysis and would like to begin a seminar, but are not sure how to deal with the practical problems of setting one up.

The first step is to become familiar with the manual itself, so that you can explain to other people what macro-analysis is all about. Brochures giving the background of the movement and a simple description of the seminars are available on request from the Philadelphia Macro-analysis Collective for you to distribute to interested people.

If you're having trouble convincing people of the importance of macro-analysis, you might want to use the essay, "Why Your Community Needs a Macro-analysis Seminar," available from the Philadelphia Macro-analysis Collective, which is written with non-radical and non-activist groups in mind. Even more respectable is the Overseas Development Council's THE U. S. & DEVELOPING WORLD: AGENDA FOR ACTION, 1974 (Praeger, N. Y., 1974), chapter VII, which pleads for macro-perspective study groups in churches, schools and community groups as one of the most responsible things they can be doing.

B. GETTING PEOPLE TOGETHER

If you are already in a group concerned with changing society in some way, for instance a peace, ecology or church group, a personal liberation group or community action project, try to interest them in doing a macro-analysis seminar. Stress the ways in which macro-analysis could be relevant and helpful to them, to give them a broader perspective; to help them decide exactly what they want to do and/or how to go about it; to overcome problems of feeling isolated, ineffective or insignificant; or to help them develop their own analysis of society and their part in it.

If the group is reluctant to take on the time commitment of a whole seminar, you might try building up interest gradually by using some of the ideas suggested in this manual in your regular meetings. The democratic group process ideas are easily applied to many situations and can do much to relieve frustration and increase effectiveness. Many of the techniques described in Chapter III can be helpful in developing and clarifying program ideas while building a "macro-analysis" perspective.

If you are not in such a group, or if your group is too small or not interested, you will have to find enough people yourself. There are numerous ways of going about this:
— Write to us in case we can put you in contact with anyone else in your area who has written to us.
— Approach people in any other local groups, such as church groups, Friends Meetings, women's and men's groups, local chapters of peace and social change organizations, and groups concerned with community issues like housing, childcare, education, etc.
— Write to your local paper, your church or community paper, explaining what macro-analysis is and asking anyone interested in get in touch with

you. Your local radio station might also be willing to help.
— Leaflet and/or put up posters in your local schools, university, churches, libraries and other likely places that have notice boards.
— Talk to people you know: at work, in your street, those you meet socially, and anyone else you come across who might be interested.
— Do a demonstration "mini" macro-analysis seminar to acquaint people with the idea and build up interest. (For more information on how to do one, see Appendix A.)

By the time you have tried some or all of these, you are likely to have discovered enough interest to get started. A seminar works best with eight to twelve participants, though six or seven will do fine if people attend regularly. It is usually best to aim for ten to fourteen starters and expect a few dropouts. If the group is much larger than that you should consider dividing into two seminars to give everybody a greater opportunity for participation.

C. PRACTICAL DETAILS

1. *Recruitment.* September is perhaps the best time to start a seminar since this is when people often make year-long time commitments. The optimum time to recruit people is either late the previous May or the first week in September. January is another good starting time. Keep in mind that many peace and social change organizations, women's and church groups plan their programs six months to a year in advance.

2. *Preparation for the first meeting.* Get the readings and the materials necessary for the seminar, keeping in mind that some literature orders can take up to six weeks to arrive. Arrange a time, date and place for the first meeting. It really helps the sessions to go well if you can meet somewhere congenial, where people can feel relaxed, and with facilities for hot drinks during the break. If possible, it is helpful to have someone who is familiar with the macro-analysis process to facilitate the first several meetings. This can be someone from the area who's been in a seminar before or perhaps a member of the macro-analysis collective, to help the group overcome the initial strangeness of the process and/or to break out of bad meeting habits. Though useful, this is not essential, and if no such person is available, just read carefully through the manual, particularly Chapter III, sections B and C on group process and Chapter III, section D on ideas for the initial meetings of a seminar.

3. *Establishing common expectations.* Everyone should be clear in advance about the commitments involved in doing a seminar: regular attendance for the duration (irregular attendance can be an even more serious problem for group morale than dropping out); two or three hours of reading and preparation between meetings; shared leadership responsibilities. It is particularly important for everyone to come to the first several meetings, since latecomers will find it difficult to become properly integrated into the group. You should also consider carefully the advantages and drawbacks of different length seminars and make a conscious decision about how long yours will last. The 12-week seminar, if conscientiously worked on by all participants, can give a fairly clear global and local perspective on current political, ecological and economic problems. Hopefully, this would help you think in terms of social change actions. Obviously the 24-week seminar is the ideal one because it will give you *time* to hear

many more different viewpoints from radical to establishment, time to develop personal trust and loving concern in your group, time to think through your own perspective. And through this time and closeness can come the ability to work out meaningful social change programs, to move toward changing your own life, and to do some education in the communities around you.

D. ENCOURAGEMENT

Organizing a seminar takes time, takes planning and takes persistence. You will undoubtedly run into snags, hassles and frustrations. But experience would indicate that it's worth it, and we would be delighted in help in any way that we can.

V. THE MACRO-ANALYSIS MOVEMENT – WHERE IT'S BEEN AND WHERE IT'S GOING

The macro-analysis movement has been growing rapidly across the United States, and now is beginning in Europe as well. A British manual has recently been written and published in London. Not only are seminars proliferating in every region of the country, but more and more people are seeking the things which the manual gives help in finding — a new and broader view of their life-situation; a new approach to analysis, vision and strategy for change, a new questioning of national ideologies, goals and structures; and adoption by their own organizations of structures and procedures which maximize democratic participation. Although spreading the 24-week-long seminar has remained the major activity of people involved in macro-analysis, different kinds of seminars with a widening audience and a variety of follow-up activities are also happening.

The macro-analysis movement can be traced back to a 1969 seminar held for social activists in metropolitan Philadelphia. The focus was economics and social change, and the group read a different book each of the fifteen weeks. The idea of seminars for Philadelphia activists continued each following year, but the issues expanded and an emphasis on democratic process and group dynamics increased. In 1971-2 there were eight seminars, all in the Philadelphia area. After the first edition of this manual (ON ORGANIZING MACRO-ANALYSIS SEMINARS) was published in August of 1972, however, macro seminars began appearing across the country. The manual has enabled new people to organize and facilitate seminars on their own where they live. During the past two years there have been almost one hundred seminars, 35 the first year of the manual and 65 this past year. In addition, other groups are using the manual for its group process suggestions and reading references. Over six thousand copies of this macro-analysis manual have been sold. In these two years the macro-analysis *movement* was born.

The seminars are being used by a variety of groups of people in social change and academic settings:
— local affiliates of national organizations, such as the American Friends Service Committee and Women's International League for Peace and Freedom.
— local church social action groups
— ad hoc groups of friends who want to do the seminar together
— college campuses, such as Stanford; Oxford, England; University of Michigan; Oberlin; Colgate; and Kalamazoo.

The seminars have also been used to help start new groups and revitalize old ones; many Movement for a New Society groups have gotten started with a macro-analysis seminar.

This manual was a necessary prerequisite for the macro-analysis movement. It helped people in Philadelphia improve their seminars by pooling the best readings and group processes into an idealized seminar so new groups could adopt the best of the different seminars, and helped avoid major pitfalls learned by experience. The writing process itself called for a much-needed gathering of information from various seminars and the sharpening up of process techniques. The manual also enabled people across the country to start their own seminars. Moreover, it has helped make the seminars more democratic because by reading the manual all the participants are at some equal minimal level of knowledge of various group procedures and techniques.

The Philadelphia Macro-analysis Collective has been vital to the spreading of macro seminars and the writing of the manual. Its role is discussed in the next section.

What do people do at the end of the seminar? Perhaps the major follow-up activity has been the organizing of new seminars. Many groups repeat the seminar for new people; many have also spawned additional, separate seminars, such as in Washington, D. C., Eugene, Philadelphia, Ann Arbor, New York, Boston, Minneapolis, The Bay Area, Baltimore and Portland. In some places macro-analysis collectives are being organized which help new seminars start locally. The spreading of the macro-analysis movement, we feel, is especially timely during this consciousness-raising period in which Americans are undergoing major re-thinking of what their country is and should be.

Many seminars have taken time out to do their own demonstrations or full-fledged campaigns as mentioned in the Introduction. However, the major activities of most seminars have not occurred within the seminar group itself, but by participants influencing other people and organizations to which they belong. Since it is hard for everyone to agree on one single new action focus, we encourage different participants to follow-up on whatever action ideas interest them with others who share that interest, rather than spending a lot of energy trying to push the whole seminar group in a single direction.

A new area into which the macro-analysis movement has branched this year has been issue-oriented seminars (see Chapter X). People who have already completed the 24-week seminar can use them to do more focused analysis, vision-building and development of action ideas in a specific issue or area in which they want to do change work. We also have helped action groups which are already focused on specific issues to develop short, issue-oriented macro-analysis seminars in order not only to analyze and construct visions and strategies on their own issues, but also to see them in a larger perspective.

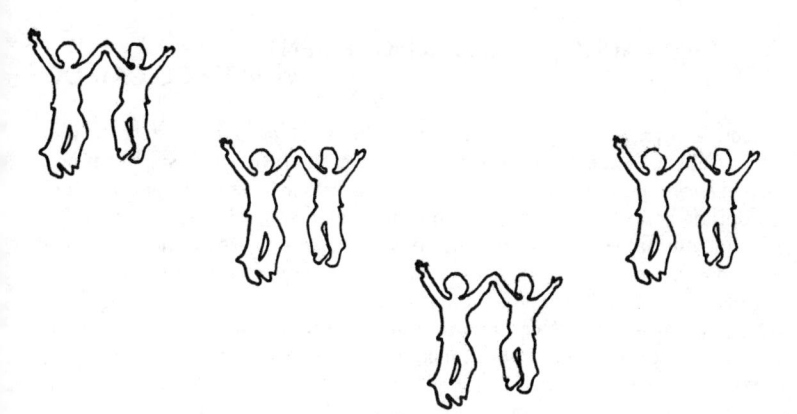

VI. THE PHILADELPHIA MACRO-ANALYSIS COLLECTIVE

The Philadelphia Macro-analysis Collective is a working group, currently of about 8 people, whose purpose is to spread the macro-analysis seminar movement and to provide support to people and groups already involved in macro-analysis. We have weekly meetings for business and sharing, using many of the same process techniques that are used in the seminars. We are open to having folks interested in macro-analysis observe our meetings.

Members of the collective wrote and revised this manual, and the collective reprints articles which would otherwise not be available for use by seminar groups, and mails out these supplies on request. We also are available to speak to groups interested in learning more about macro-analysis, help groups start seminars, and convene several seminars per year in the Philadelphia area. We keep in touch with people around the country who are interested in macro-analysis and try to direct them to others in their area who are involved with macro-analysis. In this respect we are beginning a newsletter to provide better communication among folks involved in macro-analysis. We also hope to involve other social change groups in spreading the seminars among their own constituencies.

We are a collective of the Movement for a New Society (MNS), a network of small groups across the United States dedicated to nonviolent social change. We participate in MNS programs in Philadelphia, including the two-year training program, short term training programs, and orientation weekends. A good way to get an introduction to macro-analysis and other MNS activities is to attend an orientation weekend, usually held monthly at the Philadelphia Life Center. Specific information can be obtained from the Movement for a New Society, 4722 Baltimore Avenue, Philadelphia, Pa. 19143.

VII. THE MACRO-ANALYSIS MOVEMENT: WHAT YOU CAN DO

Macro-analysis seminars are designed so that small groups can start them without outside experts. If you are part of a group involved in social action, starting a seminar together can help to broaden your perspective and focus on appropriate action, taking into account the broad range of possibilities and weighing alternatives in light of new knowledge. If you are not already part of such a group, you can start a seminar with other interested people, and you may perhaps develop into an action group.

Once you have formed a group yourself, you can help get new seminars started by talking to other folks about macro-analysis, inviting people to visit and observe your seminar, giving introductory "raps" and "mini-macros" (see Appendix A) for new groups, and perhaps attending the first few meetings of a new group to help them get started. Conferences that members of your group may attend are good places to tell potentially interested people about macro-analysis.

You or your group could also act as a contact for your area so that people interested in finding out more about macro-analysis would be in touch with you. A group might decide to become another macro-analysis collective, either performing collective functions for your area or taking on specific jobs within the macro-analysis movement, and perhaps joining the Movement for a New Society. At this writing, there is such a collective in the process of formation in Albany, New York.

Communication is also important. Different groups develop new ideas which work well, and have suggestions for new readings, improvements in the seminars which other groups can use and which can be incorporated in later versions of the manual. Send these ideas along for inclusion in the newsletter so we can all benefit from each other's experiences.

VIII. MACRO-ANALYSIS AT THE UNIVERSITY

Macro-analysis seminars of various shapes and sizes are spreading rapidly in university settings. They have been started at Stanford, Colgate, Ann Arbor, Kalamazoo, Earlham and at a number of other institutions and counter institutions. Macro-analysis combines a radical process with radical information, though these strengths create both challenges and problems for traditional education. Breaking down the student-teacher relationship may be accomplished in form through the macro-analysis process, but the idea of needing an "expert" may be a more difficult mindset to overcome. The notion of combining learning with taking action also creates some conflicts in university settings. Students often have a problem thinking in terms of action because of their short-term commitment to the class and often to the community in which they live.

Different forms of macro-analysis have been developed for differing needs of students and profs. Many seminars have been initiated by students through "experimental colleges" and "free universities," while others have been done with the professor as convenor and with required papers. When seminars have been done for credit, some participants have found that the grading process, in which a teacher evaluates a student, conflicts with the macro-analysis process in which all participants are equals. A non-graded or pass/fail system might be preferable, but if grades are necessary, self-evaluation and grading may be an acceptable solution.

In some seminars university groups have used the macro-analysis process while incorporating new readings. Others have taken the seminar readings and incorporated them into the normal classroom situation. One professor restructured his seminar to include a section on diagnosis of societal problems including the participant's relation to the problem (for instance, class and social background). This helped participants get a clearer understanding of the differences that arose between people in the seminar. Another seminar was held by a mixed group of students, professors, and townspeople. This brought some good sharing between "town" and "gown" as well as a broader perspective on social change issues.

It is clear that the macro-analysis seminars can be a useful tool in university settings. If you would like to be put in touch with people in your area who have started university seminars or with people in similar situations to your own, please write to the Philadelphia Macro-analysis Collective. An article entitled "Reschooling the Political Economy" by Bob Brownlee and Randy Gepp is also available from the collective for $.50. The paper was presented at the Mid West Economics Association and discussed macro-analysis as an important process for teaching radical economics.

Universities are an area in which macro-analysis seminars are expanding and being modified rapidly. The Macro Collective in Philadelphia would like to keep in touch with all who are using and changing the seminars so that we can better meet the needs of the university community.

IX. MACRO-ANALYSIS AND SOCIAL ACTION

A. *The need for action*
   In the introduction we stressed that macro-analysis is not an end in itself, but a means for people to take actions: actions to take charge of their own lives, and to bring about a just, democratic and safe world. The German sociologist Max Weber pointed out at the turn of the century that throughout history human societies have had extreme maldistribution of political power, of economic resources and social status. Most of the wealth, resources and power went to the relatively few people who also dominated the institutions and decision-making of the society. Virtually every reversal of this balance, every gain in human decency, justice and democracy, has been won through the efforts of people taking power through revolts, revolutions, strikes, noncooperation and other direct actions, violent and nonviolent. It is clear, however, that the many successes have failed to reverse the historical social imbalances. Not only is the gap between rich and poor widening and are the numbers of poor and hungry increasing, but the power of a super-rich minority has become more concentrated and controls ever larger sections of the world. Moreover, their pursuit of their personal interests through Industrial Growth is producing unprecedented ecological problems that threaten the future of life on this planet. Consequently, it is more imperative today than at any previous time that people act to change the balance of power and mainstream course of the human condition.

B. *SOME EXAMPLES OF ACTUAL FOLLOW-UP ACTIVITIES BY MACRO-ANALYSIS SEMINARS*

1. The macro-analysis manual and the seminar movement have evolved from the early macro-analysis seminars.
2. One of the early seminars started the campaign which prevented American ports from shipping materials to support Pakistan in its war against Bangladesh in 1971.
3. Seminar participants were shown to be social activists during the crisis at Wounded Knee in 1974. When three members of the Philadelphia Macro-analysis Collective worked with the National Council of Churches to establish a nonviolent intervention force between the AIM Indians and the government forces then threatening an Attica-like attack, they counted about a dozen of the 50 people in the intervention force who were then involved in macro-analysis seminars.
4. Many participants have started new seminars for other people and groups, as in Washington, D. C.; New York City; Grand Rapids and Ann Arbor, Mich.; Pittsburgh; and Eugene, Oregon.
5. As a result of being in a macro-analysis seminar people are increasingly involved in opposition to atomic energy plants. A particularly active campaign was begun in Portland, Oregon, during the Summer of 1974 which included a 100-mile march to a plant site with leafleting, public meetings and much publicity.
6. A Palo Alto, California, seminar, with help from the American Friends Serv-

ice Committee, wrote a manual on simple living entitled, "Taking Charge." It helps people relate worldwide political, economic and ecological conditions to their own consumptive life style, and reduce their consumption to more equitable levels. The booklet has been adopted as a reading in the macro-analysis seminars.

7. A New York State macro seminar group meets twice a week: once to hold their seminar and once to do some kind of nonviolent action.

8. A seminar in Butte, Montana facilitated the organization of a food coop with more than 100 families, and a film forum showing political films grew out of that.

9. A macro seminar group in Berea, Kentucky got the local City Council to endorse a state-wide bottle return bill, and sponsored local Sun Day celebrations featuring displays on alternatives to nuclear energy.

10. A group in Salt Lake City, Utah began a successful "guerilla gardening" project on the parking strips along the roads owned by the City, and significantly raised people's consciousness about control of their food supplies being in the hands of multinational corporations.

11. Many people have changed their lifestyles and eating habits, quit oppressive jobs, and now work more intensely for social change because of their participation in macro-analysis seminars.

C. SOME TYPES OF FOLLOW-UP ACTIVITIES YOUR MACRO-ANALYSIS SEMINAR MIGHT CONSIDER

1. *Start New Seminars.* Help organizations with which you are involved to convene macro-analysis seminars, or convene a macro-analysis seminar for your friends and neighbors who may be looking for new ways to become involved in social action. This is a very important action for social change, since seminars are spread primarily through this kind of multiplication. The seminar might also be modified to appeal to specific groups; e.g., high school students, minority groups, occupational groups, etc. Ideally each macro seminar should generate two new seminars.

2. *Research-Study-Action Projects.* Some groups may choose a broad topic such as ecology, energy, or imperialism for more in-depth study before getting involved in specific social action. Others may be ready to begin an action project on a specific problem and incorporate ongoing research and study into their campaign plans. Many action groups, such as anti-B-1 Bomber and nuclear energy opposition groups began with issue-oriented seminars in which they developed a better analysis, vision, strategy and action ideas on their concerns before launching too far into social action campaigns. (See Chapter X on Issue Oriented Seminars) The process and methodology of macro seminars are useful to such groups. The study-action group might also be oriented around creating an economic or political alternative to an oppressive structure.

3. *Work With an Organization.* Seminar members might focus on groups to which they already belong, or join with a good existing social change group. They can examine the principles and program of the group from a macro perspective and assist in developing analysis, vision and strategy for change as well as action programs for the organization.

X. ISSUE-ORIENTED SEMINARS

A. INTRODUCTION

The issue oriented seminar gives a group an opportunity to focus in more depth on a specific subject using the macro-analysis perspective and group process tools. It can be used at the end of a regular 24 or 12 week seminar for further study of a particular issue, in preparation for action in that area, or by existing action groups needing background for developing a campaign. There are several advantages in going through a regular seminar first:
- It gives a group a common background of thinking in analysis, vision, and strategy.
- It provides grounding in the big picture of social problems so that a specific issue can be seen in a broader context.
- It helps people avoid being trapped by short-sighted or tunnel-visioned solutions.
- It provides experience in functioning together that can make groups more democratic, meetings more efficient and enjoyable, and actions that grow out of it more effective.

There will be some situations, however, perhaps with action groups that are already functioning and operating under time pressure, in which it makes sense to start out immediately with an issue-oriented seminar. But it is particularly important for these groups to start out with some readings that provide a big picture perspective before getting to their own issue.

B. CHOOSING A SUBJECT

There are infinite possibilities — any report in the seminar could be expanded into months of study. But there's no need to be arbitrary. Below are several questions to ask in making the decision:
- Is it something that's important to the people involved? More than just a theoretical exercise?
- Can the learning be applied to your daily life?
- Is it an issue that's facing people in your area? Is it something that can be organized around?

If you're still having trouble choosing, pick several likely issues, construct web charts or force field analyses to relate them to the rest of society and brainstorm questions for research. This might help raise the potential or drawbacks of different issues.

C. SETTING UP THE SEMINAR FORMAT

Keep in mind the general macro process — wide participation in information-giving, egalitarian group process, inclusion of vision, strategy and action thinking as well as analysis. (If you haven't done so already, read Chapter IV of this manual.) A possible format to build on is suggested below:

2 sessions — introduction: choosing the subject; grounding in where people are coming from, through personal oppressions, personal sharing of goals, etc.; choosing readings to provide broad perspective and analysis of the issue.

3 sessions — reports and discussion on that material.

2 sessions — reports and discussion on visions and vision building relating to that issue.

2 sessions — strategy & action: readings such as the "Direct Action Mini-Manual"; brainstorming questions; strategy games; building a possible campaign. (For more vision, strategy and action ideas, see Chapters VII and IX of the manual.)

Consider starting an action around an issue as you are studying it; getting involved in action raises a lot of vital questions to study, while studying suggests different approaches to action.

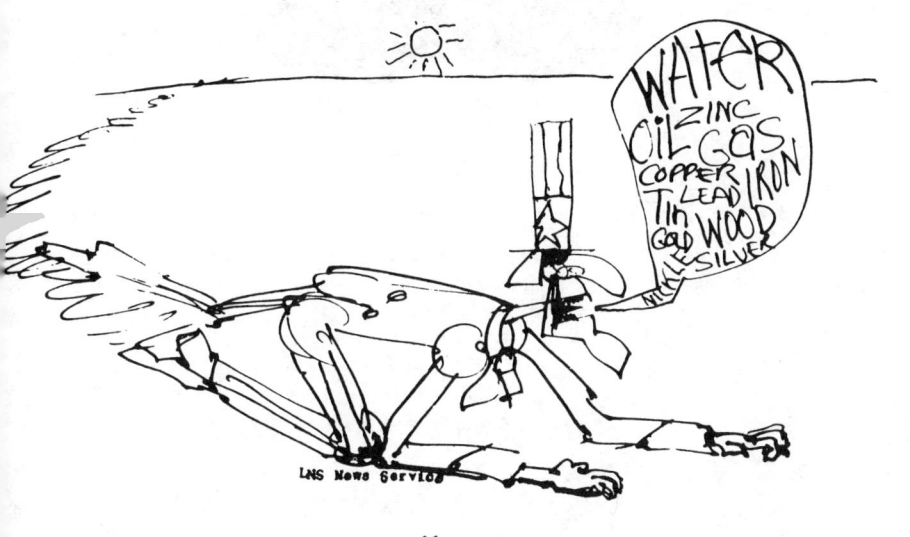

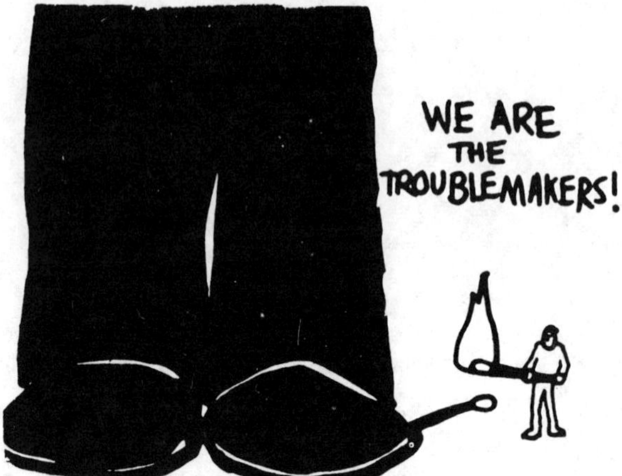
WE ARE
THE
TROUBLEMAKERS!

APPENDIX A: HOW TO DO A "MINI-MACRO"

A "mini-macro" is a one-session demonstration macro-analysis seminar intended to introduce people to macro-analysis content and process.

A. AGENDA

An agenda for a 2½ - 3 hour mini-macro might look like this:

Personal introductions (if the group members do not already know each other)	5
Excitement sharing (introductions and excitement sharing can be combined)	5
Agenda Review	5
Introduction of macro-analysis by the facilitator	15
Distribute articles for reports	5
Reading time	20
Reports and discussion	35 - 50
Break	10
Relating material to social change action	35 - 50
Discussion of macro - questions and answers	15
Evaluation	5

B. PROCESS

Most of these agenda items are handled exactly as they are in a beginning or regular seminar session.

It has been our experience that groups doing a mini-macro often do not have an opportunity before the session to read articles to report on. Therefore, we schedule reading time during the session. If a group can do the readings beforehand, this should be omitted.

Reading materials can be distributed so that each person reads a different article (although there probably would not be time for everyone to do a report). However, some of us have found it more effective to use just four or five articles, so that each article is read by at least two people. One person would give the report and others who have read the same article can add to it. Be sure to keep to time limits on the reports and urge people to report on the points in the articles which were important to them rather than trying to summarize the article.

Reading materials which present a subject in relation to the broad perspective should be chosen.   **If you need advice or materials, contact John Koch, Department of Economics, Blackburn College, Carlinville, IL 62626.**

Throughout a mini-macro it is important to keep in mind its demonstration nature and be explicit about this with the group. Process is perhaps even more important than content in this situation, since the subject matter is often arbitrary. Special attention should be paid to equal participation, time limits and explaining why each agenda item is being done. Issues about process should be raised during evaluation.

APPENDIX B: UNDERLYING PRINCIPLES OF MACRO-ANALYSIS

Because the principles, values, and assumptions that underlie macro-analysis are scattered throughout this manual, and some are only stated implicitly, we want to bring them all together in one place and make them explicit.

In addition to making these principles clear, this appendix should be valuable for several other reasons. It should help seminar conveners and participants make changes if they want to (1) agree that a certain principle is good and innovate in how to apply it; (2) lay aside a principle and develop an alternative and practical ways of implementing it; or (3) incorporate new principles and ways of implementing them. All of these are fine as long as the innovators are clear about what they are doing. It is important to be really familiar with the various procedures and techniques and the part they play in implementing the guiding principles before trying to change them.

Lastly, while we're pleased that an extremely diverse range of individuals and groups have found some particular dimension of macro-analysis to be of use (e.g., the bibliography, group process suggestions, or the study-to-action procedures), we hope that a familiarity with these underlying principles will enable users of the manual to decide for themselves whether what they're doing is really macro-analysis or whether it is different enough to be better described as something else.

All of this is not to discourage creativity. This appendix is intended to help folks understand the functions played by various topics, procedures, etc., and the probable effect of dropping or changing them, so as to be in a better position to decide what changes to make. Inadequately thought-out changes can leave a seminar group seriously disoriented or damage its morale.
Although that kind of learning can be valuable, there will be many instances when we can build on the experience of previous seminars instead of repeating it.

These principles are very much open to change and expansion. The entire macro-analysis process is always experimental, changing in response to the cumulative experience of more than 200 seminars in the past three years. An example of change is the increasingly apparent importance of seminar groups encouraging a positive, hopeful, mutually self-affirming and trusting attitude among participants. Why? Because a major goal of macro-analysis is helping people become more effective social change agents, and people who have become seriously depressed by concentrating on a "hard-headed" analysis of the "hopeless" world situation are not likely to accomplish that goal.

Here, then, are the principles which, to date, have been important in defining what a macro-analysis seminar is. Following each principle are the reasons it is considered important, and a description of the procedures useful in implementing it.

A. GROUP PROCESS
1. *The maintenance of participatory democracy in all the activities of the seminar group is vital.* This is so for many reasons, two very important ones being (1) participatory democracy is a crucial part of our vision of a better society, and we will best achieve that by practicing it now at every possible opportunity; and (2) the evidence of many macro seminars, especially when contrasted with standard high school and college learning situations, is that people learn faster and more effectively, and are more likely to move on to social change applications of their learning, when they are in charge of the learning situation.

Participatory democracy is maintained primarily through procedures that encourage (1) equal participation in the seminar, and (2) equal sharing within the group of the power and information necessary for decision-making. Equal participation is aided by: everyone's ownership of, and familiarity with, the macro manual; regular rotation of the role of facilitator; and an agenda which is on a large sheet of paper in view of everyone and which is reviewed each meeting and open to changes suggested by any participant. Procedures encouraging equal participation include: several occasions on which the person speaking is not to be interrupted, including report giving, brainstorming, and "think and listen"; and the availability of exercises to raise the consciousness of people who tend to speak too frequently (e.g., giving up one of a small number of allotted matches each time one speaks, and not being permitted to speak when one's matches are gone); the reports format in which each person has the opportunity to contribute information; and agenda items like excitement sharing which include everyone.

2. *Participants need to get to know each other more deeply than just in the limited role of co-learners.* If group members come to trust and appreciate each other more and more as the seminar goes on, the seminar will be a more enjoyable experience; the group will come to mean more to each participant; more effective learning will occur, because people will feel trustful enough of the group to share ideas they aren't really sure about; participants are more likely to develop social action plans that will really be meaningful and implementable; and the quality of meetings will improve, because everyone will really care about giving good reports, being an alert facilitator, timekeeper, etc.

Procedures which encourage this deepening level of trust include the values clarification exercises and other structured sharing in the introductory sessions of the seminar; excitement sharing, and occasional extended excitement sharing; potluck meals together, etc. (see Appendix D on community building.)

3. *All of us can develop a kind of learning/teaching experience that is empowering* to us because we will grow in our reliance on and respect for our ability both to think clearly and to successfully tackle problems, rather than concluding that only the "experts" know enough to act on these issues. This principle breaks down into two more specific ones: (3A) *Each group knows*

best what its own unique needs are. Repeatedly throughout the manual options are presented for alternative ways to deal with a specific topic, situation, need, etc. Each group should assess its own needs, and then determine how best to meet them in the context of the overall seminar structure. (3B) *Each group needs to keep doing the things that will build a solid, authentic sense of achievement, and the things that will help it recognize and appreciate what it is achieving.* Procedures important in producing this sense of achievement include: (a) Careful adherence to suggested time limits. If each report is finished on time, there will be time in the session to relate new information to social change, *and* the session will finish on time. These achievements in turn lead to finishing topics as expected, creating a ongoing sense of momentum and achievement. If reports are repeatedly too long, sessions will run overtime, etc., and a sense of failure can easily set i (b) Sensitivity in judging how much time is worth allotting to completely open-ended discussion. Participants in many seminars have found it frustrating and unproductive to discuss at length points for which documenting information is not at hand. Similarly, it can be very unsatisfy to get off on tangents and not end up where you wanted to be. (c) Being careful to allow significant amounts of time for relating information to soci change. This may seem unimportant if action ideas generated aren't acted immediately, but is in fact valuable first because participants will usually take these ideas back into their own lives, and into other groups they're involved in, e.g., ecology, peace, social justice. Secondly, generating idea for social change and reviewing them periodically reminds the group of all things that could be done; this is an important counter-balance to the depressing nature of much of the information the reports bring to light. Thi review of action ideas also reminds the group how much it has accomplishe (d) Sensitivity in making efficient use of overall session time, but not overburdening the group. Work toward finding your own group's balance betwe the amount of information input and discussion that feels positive and exci ing, and the amount that feels too intense and overwhelming.

4. *Doing enjoyable, energizing things to help keep group morale and energy level high is very important.* Precisely because macro seminars have a very serious purpose we need energy from many sources. One is the attainment and appreciation of solid achievement described above; another is the combination of excitement sharing, singing, stretches, and active games which can be inserted at low-energy points in a seminar session. These raise our energy level for more creative work, release tension, and help us to start implementing now a vision of a society in which people enjoy each other through work and play.

5. *Regular carrying out of effective evaluations.* This principle is placed at t end of the group process section because in some ways it encompasses al the previous principles. An evaluation that is both frank and honest, and at the same time sensitive and supportive of seminar participants, is a crucial mechanism for sharing everyone's assessment of how well things are going

in all the previous areas, and making use of the collective wisdom of the group in making improvements for the future. It is the major opportunity to implement the process of molding the seminar structure to meet the group's particular needs; and to strengthen group trust and increase energy by reflecting on things that went well.

B. TOPICS

6. *Maintenance of the cumulative nature of the information shared in the seminar.* This is important for two major reasons. First, the study of a set of topics which have been arranged to stress their inter-relatedness helps people build a sense of things falling into place which the study of a random series of topics usually doesn't produce. This excitement helps maintain a high level of enthusiasm about the seminar. Secondly, the topics are arranged logically in terms of the constraints they put upon possible solutions to the problems. Thus it is important to discuss ecology first, because the limits of the physical world are the widest and most final ones to be kept in mind. So a seminar group that feels a need to change the order of, add, or delete topics should try to assess the probable effect of the change on the cumulative nature of the seminar.

7. *Subtopics studied are geared to action.* Action for social change is, of course, the major purpose of macro-analysis seminars. New subtopics which a group is considering investigating should be assessed with the goal of determining how their study will strengthen efforts for social change.

C. READINGS

8. *An emphasis on readings, both those in the manual and new ones added by groups, that go to the roots of problems.* The vast majority of readings included advocate fundamental social change in our political and economic systems. The readings chosen are biased this way for two reasons: first, this fundamental change perspective is one which is usually not well known, whereas we are all constantly immersed, via the various media, in various shorter range reform arguments as well as arguments denying that the things we study are problems at all. Secondly, the case for fundamental change is a sound one, with which social change activists should be familiar for many reasons stated over and over again throughout the manual. Participants may want to include more examples of other viewpoints so that several perspectives can be examined side-by-side.

9. At least some of the new readings a group introduces on any subtopic should include *new knowledge* (readings which go to the roots of problems); proposed *values* or guidelines with which to approach the subject; proposals for *solutions*; and ideas about *strategy* for making the solutions happen. "Going to the roots of a problem" means raising questions about what is really necessary to solve the problem, and not stopping short of that because of vested interests which would be threatened if a true resolution of the problem came about.

10. Readings should go deeply enough into each subtopic to point to at least some *links between ostensibly different topics.*

D. ACTION

11. *A small group of people, such as the participants in a macro-analysis seminar, can undertake meaningful and successful social action toward the resolution of some of the problems confronted.*

12. *The success of a seminar should be evaluated primarily on the basis of influence on our actions for social change and on our personal lives.* As suggested earlier, this can take several forms besides that of the seminar group deciding to do an action project together. These can include personal lifestyle changes, the introduction of new ideas to other social change groups, organizing new seminars, and other ideas mentioned in Chapter X the manual.

13. *We are all victims of the problems we are studying,* not altruistic social reformers working on someone else's problems. This should be kept in mind as we consider how to tackle problems and work toward solutions. In almost all cases, some study and reflection indicate that these problems affect us personally and are not just abstract subjects. The better we understand that and look upon our action as the opportunity to improve the quality of our own lives, the more strength we will have to draw on in the struggle.

APPENDIX C: EMPOWERMENT—SOME THEORY & TOOLS

A. INTRODUCTION
We have been very successful in the macro-analysis movement in finding ways of taking power over our own learning process, and this manual has been helpful in providing specific information and tools that enable groups of people to do that. We have been less successful, however, in providing ways to help people take the leap from reflection to action. While ideally the seminars provide people with the information they need to take action to change their environment, in practice many people end up feeling more knowledgeable, but frustrated, inadequate and even less powerful as a result.

There are some broad historical reasons why less direct action is coming out of seminars these days. Two factors present during the early seminars' years and no longer present seem to be relevant. The first is that the large size and cohesion of the civil rights and anti-war movement of the late sixties provided a secure base from which to act. Many people who didn't usually think in terms of nonviolent direct action grew brave as the intensity of the effort mounted and were able to join in direct action campaigns. The second is that both movements were on high visibility issues and were working toward goals that were concrete and easily understandable, at least on a superficial level. Since then, the issues have multiplied and become more diffuse and hard to dramatize. Consequently many people are now discouraged and inactive who had previously been swept along with the tide.

But the issue is a larger one. The enormity of the changes needed at the social level makes it hard for us to relate to them no matter how clearly focused. And while we can see and begin to act on the personal changes that need to happen, we tend when we evaluate the seminar to discount those changes, to apologize for their insignificance, and to emphasize instead all the things that didn't happen. Clearly, we need to develop a more balanced perspective on action—both to recognize the value of personal change as a necessary and legitimate part of social change, and to understand the obstacles that stand in the way of taking action against societal evils. Then, rather than feeling guilty, we can fully appreciate the action that *does* come out of seminars and build on that experience to do even better.

What can be said in this manual that will help people to do that, to take control of the information and come out feeling more empowered than when they went in? The Philadelphia Macro-Analysis Collective spent the thinking time of our weekly meetings during the winter and spring of 1975 working toward an answer to that question.

We started out with ourselves—thinking about what motivates us to take action in the first place, what we need to be able to take charge of difficult situations, how we approach making the changes that we want to make. It was exciting to get that kind of immediate personal grounding. It taught us a great deal about the most basic elements of empowerment and helped to make clear the kinds of things that seminar participants could do to act mo effectively on the information they receive. This appendix is a synthesis of some of those insights. Section B expands on the general theory of empow erment; Section C includes specific tools and things people can do in seminars in this area; and Section D mentions some resources that might b helpful.

B. THEORY OF EMPOWERMENT

The most fundamental way of taking power over the information in a macro-analysis seminar is to integrate it into our own life experience, to se how we fit into that big picture. We are learning that the most lasting socia change comes in areas where we have not only a sound intellectual analysi of the situation but also some personal interest or concern—where the change really makes a difference to us. One macro seminar at the Universit of Michigan put together an additional section for the seminar on this topi which they introduced with the following:

"Each of us is essential to macro-analysis. Our own personal situation a perspective has definite implications for how we define and carry out personal and social change. Individual interests and their collective bases major ingredients in understanding and developing goals for change. A ma part of this process is understanding where we have been and how this affects where we want to go. Each of us is a product of our own history, an factors such as race, sex, ideology, class, and ethnicity have an influence who we are. Personal and collective exploration of our social roots is a mea to determine our own and other seminar members' self-interest in relation ship to social change."

We also need to have a "macro" perspective on power, to understand ho is presently distributed and how that can be changed. We have come to tak our powerlessness very much for granted in this society. We often forget t there is an alternative. Yet the power of nearly any system comes ultimatel from people's willingness to put up with it—to recognize its authority, obe its laws, respect its expertise, subordinate their own opinions, preference and priorities to what they perceive to be the demands of the larger group (though in many systems, those demands are created by a powerful elite a are not in the real interests of the majority). This willingness to relinquish power can be developed and maintained in many ways—by threat of force, an absence of visible alternatives, by the myth that participation in decision-making presently exists, by the myth of expertise that keeps us from challenging people in positions of authority, by creation of a sense o individual powerlessness.

Our power over our own lives and our sense of our own worth are dimin ished in other ways by the political and economic system. A profitable and expansive market economy requires the creation of artificial needs for goo which distorts our values and obstructs our ability to recognize and meet r human needs. Advertising, in order to increase sales, drums home the me sage that we're not good enough as we are. Our sense of isolation and alienation is fostered by the atmosphere of competition and divisiveness in which no one can be trusted, one person can gain success or privilege only at the expense of another, and a feeling of self-worth is acquired by having somebody else to look down on.

All of these ways of maintaining power, profit and privilege are threatened when people begin to discover that they can take charge of their lives—that they can love and be loved for who they are, that they know what they really need, that they are smart, capable of understanding, making good decisions, taking responsibility, and following through with action. Since our system is inherently irrational in terms of meeting human needs, any effectively loving and rational person in this society would have to end up being a revolutionary. Reclaiming our own power and our own humanity, therefore, whenever and wherever we can, and helping others to do the same, is basic to any other social change work that we do.

We are all at different stages of being able to take charge of our personal or political world. But whether it is helping a meeting to function democratically, or responding to higher prices by organizing a food co-op, or occupying the site of a nuclear power plant to prevent it from being built, all are important to make a next step possible. Any step, no matter how small, that helps us develop a mind-set of being able to act on situations instead of reacting to them significantly increases our ability to participate in and even organize efforts to bring about social change on a larger scale. Through that sense of empowerment we can begin to relearn and indeed invent the tools for developing the self-reliance and the support that are needed in the struggle to transform society.

C. TOOLS

The tools listed below are ones we in the Philadelphia Macro-Analysis Collective have created, borrowed and adapted to use in our own thinking about empowerment, and have found helpful enough to be worth sharing.

1. *Sharing Thinking.* Often just the simple process of taking time in a group for each person to think about an issue, then share that thinking, can generate a wealth of insights and information and exciting new ideas. It seems a particularly good way of applying our own experience to larger issues and making new connections between them. This "think and listen" process described below can be used with four to twelve people, and time for each step can be adjusted according to the overall time available and the number of people in the group. Following the description is a list of topics that lend themselves to thinking about empowerment.

a. A particular issue is chosen which everyone focuses on. People in the group spend time thinking by themselves with pen and paper (this time can be taken either before or during the meeting). OPTION: Divide in twos and have one person think aloud for a designated amount of time while the other listens silently, maybe taking notes for the person who is thinking, then reverse roles. The attention of another person can stimulate new thinking, and the process can help people to organize and articulate the important points before sharing them with the group. Not having any feedback from t listener is important in creating a safe environment just for thinking.

b. After the designated amount of time, people return to the group prepared to share their thinking. The amount of time available for this step divided equally among each of the participants. Each individual shares her/his thinking with the group with a short time at the end for clarifying questions. (This is also a good process tool for groups that are having diffi culties with unequal participation.)

c. Time should be set aside at the end for group discussion. Finding com mon threads in people's sharing and isolating important factors helps to incorporate the personal thinking into group thinking.

Suggested topics:

a. *Growing up.* Realizing that people's values and their understanding of their role in society are greatly influenced by experiences which they had while growing up, exploring some of this past can help illuminate the prese situation. Some questions that might be useful to think about are: When yc were young who did you feel superior to? Who did you feel inferior to? Wha were you expected to do or be when you grew up? How did you react to tho expectations? Where did your motivation for social change come from?

b. *Taking charge.* The purpose of this exercise is to isolate factors which help people to take action, and factors which hold them back. During the thinking time, each person thinks of times or situations in which they were able to take action, make changes, or feel in control of a difficult situation (standing up to somebody, challenging authority, changing jobs, getting a group to do something, making a stand, altering lifestyle, etc.), and think c the factors which enabled them to take that action. The process can be repeated with people thinking about the times when it was hard to take acti and the factors involved in that. With a list of the variety of factors that help and hinder in making changes, the group can begin to get a broader perspective on the most basic things that we need in order to make any kin of change.

c. *Strategy.* Having everyone in the seminar write their own strategy for large scale social change really encourages people to do some broad thinking. This tool can help people to look carefully at what they are doing and how it fits in with their strategy for social change. A helpful way of thinking about it is to project into the future: "By the year 2000 we are living in the kind of society that we would like to see. What were the steps that we necessary to bring that about?" (or choose a shorter time span and a more limited goal). Enough thinking is required for this that preparation is probably best done before the meeting.

2. *Sharing Success Stories.* Looking at the experience of people who have successfully managed to bring about changes can be an encouragement to thinking about taking action. Gene Sharp's POLITICS OF NONVIOLENT ACTION (1973) is full of success stories. Personal experiences of

successful action are also very good to share.

3. *Brainstorming Reasons Why It's All Hopeless.* The purpose of this exercise is to air the feelings of hopelessness that often keep people from taking action; to recognize the existence of those feelings and deal with them openly instead of thinking they shouldn't be there or pretending they aren't. The group starts by brainstorming all the reasons why it feels hopeless (either a specific action, or social change in general), then picks one or more of those reasons and figures out specific things that can be done to overcome that sense of hopelessness.

4. *Problem-solving.* A good way to gain experience in finding solutions to problems and acting on them is to practice. Below are two different approaches to problem solving that individuals and groups involved in social change have found helpful.

   a. Group problem solving. Bring in some practical problems to solve in the second half of the seminar session—either a situation an individual is facing or a local issue that needs dealing with. Have one person introduce the problem and another one facilitate and record. Start with the first person clearly stating the problem, with a few sentences of history and any solutions that have already been tried. Then have the group brainstorm approaches to solutions (a good way of surfacing really creative possibilities is to phrase them in terms of "goal-wishes"—"I wish that..." "How could we...?"). After about five minutes, the person who introduced the problem picks one of those ideas (or combines several) to work on further, starting out by saying three positive things about it, then one area that needs more thought. The group then brainstorms on that area and the process is repeated until the time is up (about a half hour is good) and/or the person has a clear idea of possible next steps in working toward a solution. Important elements in this style of problem solving are quickness, unfettered creativity, enthusiasm, and building on positive ideas.

   b. Individual problem solving. This is an exercise to help people think in an organized and concrete way about strategy for acting on a particular issue—what the present situation is, what the desired one would be, what things stand in the way of that happening, and what steps can be taken to overcome those blocks. The format outlined below can help people organize that information. The issue can range from personal goals (where my life is now and where I'd like it to be in a year) to strategies for a campaign someone is involved with. A good way to use this exercise in a seminar is to introduce it, then have each person work individually for about half an hour, then gather together, either in small groups or as a whole, to share insights.

PRESENT SITUATION	← forces keeping me in present	BLOCKS	forces moving me toward goal →	DESIRED SITUATION

People who would be affected by change:
_____
_____
_____

Specific steps to take to overcome blocks:
_____
_____
_____

D. RESOURCES

As the collective thought together on empowerment, in addition to our own experience, we found a variety of readings helpful, ranging from Erich Fromm's THE ART OF LOVING to Paulo Freire's PEDAGOGY OF THE OPPRESSED; from Abraham Maslow's personality theory to the theory of Re-evaluation Counseling (see Appendix D). We encourage others to draw their own experience and knowledge of other resources to stimulate and enrich their thinking on the whole issue of empowerment.

APPENDIX D: MORE RESOURCES

This appendix is intended to better help groups in different situations to tailor the macro-analysis experience to their own needs. Aside from the specific issues that people might want to study (mentioned in the body of the manual), we've though of five areas which different groups might be feeling special needs to spend time focusing on: A) how to build community and support within a group; B) how to work more effectively in groups; C) how to develop skills in personal growth; D) how to do direct action; and E) how to research a local community. For each of these areas we suggest: 1) how you might tell whether that is a need of your group (just in case you don't already know); 2) some ideas of things you might do; 3) other resources to go to.

A. COMMUNITY BUILDING

For a good group (either this macro group or another you're involved in) with potential for doing all sorts of good things, but one in which people don't know each other well enough or don't feel cohesive enough to function well together. An important reason why many groups find it hard to move from study to action is this sense of distance and lack of enough trust—spending some time developing that sense of community may, therefore, be very vital and basic social change work.

Ideas and tools:

— Spend more time on the kinds of things suggested for the introductory sessions of a seminar (pp. 14-22).
— Share on different questions like childhood memories, reactions to injustice, feelings of oppression, the origin of your motivation for social change, etc. (Think of the appropriate ones for your group—and make the questions as specific as possible.) A good format to use is the "think and listen" in which time is evenly divided among all the participants (it can be done in the whole group or in several smaller ones, or even in pairs) and each person thinks out loud on that subject for the duration of the time (2-5 minutes, usually) while the other(s) listens. It is particularly important that the listener(s) do just that, and not comment on the thinking, interject personal experiences, initiate discussion, or even ask questions. This helps establish an atmosphere of safety where people can feel free to share things that may be too personal, tentative, seemingly unimportant, or otherwise scary to come out in regular discussion.
— Do other things together—potluck suppers; outings; celebrations with singing, dancing, and sharing things you've created; co-operative games during meeting breaks; shopping? childcare? others? (brainstorm the possibilities). Expand the levels on which you interact with and know each other.

- Rotate meetings among different houses to get more of a feel for what each others' lives are like.
- Spend time regularly appreciating each other (like after excitement sharing, tell something you particularly like about the person on your left). Most of us find this awkward to do because it's embarassing and because we are so conditioned to look for faults, to put ourselves and everybody else down. As a result, lots of things we really like about people go unsaid and everybody's sense of confidence and self-worth is needlessly diminished. It's exciting to see the dynamic reversed as people begin building on the positive.
- Approach conflicts within the group as a challenge and an opportunity for growth. Practice conflict resolution skills.
- Do group problem solving—like each week spend half an hour applying your accumulated wisdom to a practical problem of a different member of the group (see Appendix C, section on Tools).
- Take some time at the end of each meeting to share personal goals for the coming week, then report back on them.
- Share visions of community.
- Think of things you would like to be able to do personally, but can't for lack of support—see if others can help.
- Do self-estimation (good for ongoing groups where trust level is already fairly high, as a way of getting thoughtful feedback on individuals in relation to the group). Each person takes some time to tell what they see as their strengths in that group and ways in which they would like to grow. Others then have the opportunity to respond, using the same format. Careful phrasing of the second part ("A way that I would wish for you to grow...") is particularly important if people are to really hear criticism. It's also helpful to allow some quiet time at the beginning of each self-estimation so that people can think out what they want to say.

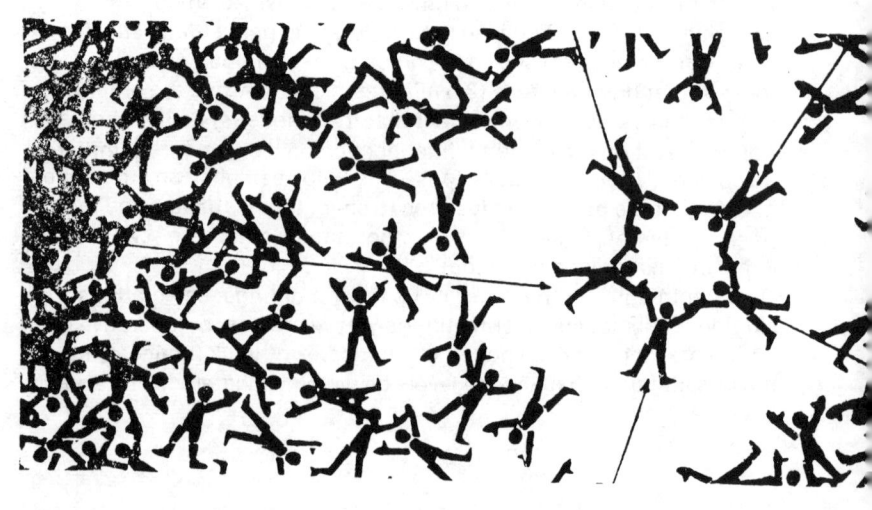

RESOURCES

RESOURCE MANUAL FOR A LIVING REVOLUTION, alias "the monster manual," Virginia Coover, et al., (available from New Society Publishers $8.95 postpaid). 330 pages of resources and tools for trainers/organizers in nonviolent social change. Good sections on community building, values clarification, and conflict resolution.

BUILDING SOCIAL CHANGE COMMUNITIES, Training/Action Affinity Group (New Society Publishers, $4.95 postpaid). Sections on forming communities, meeting facilitation, consensus decision-making, creative conflict resolution, networks and more!

A MANUAL ON NONVIOLENCE AND CHILDREN, Stephanie Judson, et al. (Available from New Society Publishers, $8.95 postpaid). Includes a full section called "For the Fun of It: Selected Cooperative Games for Children and Adults" of great use. Also good thinking about how people learn in group situations.

VALUES CLARIFICATION, Sidney B. Simon, et al. (NY: Hart Publishing Co., (1972). A lot of specific exercises to help individuals and groups understand where their basic values lie.

CLEARNESS: PROCESS FOR SUPPORTING INDIVIDUALS AND GROUPS IN DECISION-MAKING, Peter Woodrow (New Society Publishers, $2.25 postpaid). Helps break down individual isolation in making important decisions about one's life, work, family, community.

A MANUAL FOR GROUP FACILITATORS, Brian Auvine et al., (Available from New Society Publishers, $5.50 postpaid). Helps individuals think well about groups and communities they are starting, training, aiding.

LEADERSHIP FOR CHANGE, Lakey & Kokopeli (New Society Publishers, $2.25 postpaid). Feminist view of leadership helps people think about specific task and morale leadership functions which must be performed in any group for it to succeed.

B. GROUP PROCESS

For a group that is having trouble functioning effectively, wants to develop further its members' skills in group process, or wants to think about how to apply what its members know about groups to other groups of which they a part. Some common problems are: interrupting; people not listening while others are talking but rather thinking of what they want to say next; no space between comments so that people don't have time to think and have to compete to get a word in edgewise; unequal participation (some people— often men in this culture—talking a lot and others hardly saying anything) authoritarian facilitation; dragginess; unfocused discussion. Probably every group faces some of these problems at one time or another. What is important is to realize that they do not have to be allowed to continue, but that there are things that can be done to deal with them and improve the overall functioning of the group.

Ideas and tools:

1. Sometimes the exact problem in a group is not clear and the first task is identify the problem(s). One possible way to go about this is to:
   — Have each person share 1) ways in which they feel good about the group 2) problems they see, and if possible, 3) suggestions for improvement List them in three columns on a big sheet of newsprint. be as specific as possible about where the problems lie.
   — Brainstorm additional possible solutions and list them on column 3.
   — Examine the possible solutions and decide on which ones to implement. Make specific plans for when and how to do it and who will take responsibility.

(This is not unlike the problem/solution/project tool suggested for relating the seminar readings to social change action.)

A good general principle to keep in mind in dealing with group process problems—and lots of other problems, too—is to build on the positive things about the group. (That's why in the process described above we suggest that each person start by saying good things.) There are two reasons for this:

— Our society tends to look at things negatively, to be quick to criticize and hesitant to praise, and if we are going to build a more positive society, we need to begin now to recognize, state and reinforce positive things. We're not accustomed to looking for these things and stating them, so it may feel awkward at first, but it can rapidly become a natural and joyous way of responding to the world around us.

— It works! A session which is focused on negatives quickly becomes depressing and discouraging, and leaves people feeling helpless about finding solutions. It may also give a false picture of the situation, making it look totally bad when, in reality, there are many positives which can be built on and specific areas which need improvement. Beginning with good things helps to put the problems that exist in their proper perspective within the overall functioning of the group and to build a positive tone where people will feel empowered to find solutions to the problems. (A good discipline in discussion in general might be always to say something positive about an idea before criticizing it.)

A group which continues to have difficulty after trying to work out their problems may want to have an outside observer attend one or more meetings to give the group feedback and participate in a problem solving session. A "group process expert" is not necessary. Any thoughtful and observant person with a fresh perspective and some knowledge of how groups function can be immensely helpful.

Regular, full use of the evaluation process can help in dealing with problems before they become major, and in checking on changes a group has agreed on to see if they are having the desired result.

2. More specific suggestions for dealing with some of the above mentioned problems follow:
— *Listening* exercises can help people focus on what has just been said. Before responding to a person, you echo back what you heard that person say; e.g., "I heard you say that..." You do not go on to make your own point until the previous speaker is satisfied that s/he has been accurately heard.
— *Unequal participation* is often blamed on the people in a group who are quiet when often, in fact, the problem is that a few people are talking so often and long that there is no space for those who are less aggressive or quick thinking. An effective method of raising consciousness about how often people speak is to give everyone an equal number of matches (or whatever) and have people throw one into the center of the room each time they speak. When a person runs out of matches, s/he can no longer talk. If length of talking is a problem, try having people light the match as they start talking. When they can no longer hold it, time is up! Exercises like this seem awkward, and some are not meant to be used on a long term basis, but they can be very helpful for raising awareness about participation in the group.
— Another method which can be used on many occasions for equalizing participation and eliminating the problem of *people thinking of what they want to say next instead of listening* is to take a minute or two for everyone to collect their thoughts on the subject, then go around the room, giving each person an equal amount of time to share their thinking. If people really don't have anything to contribute, they should be given the option of passing. But time and again those who have been defined as not having much to say have valuable contributions to make if they do not have to compete to get a word in edgewise.
— A method which has been useful during brainstorming when a few people seem to be *dominating* is to have those who are contributing a lot to the brainstorm wait 10 seconds after the last speaker while

people who are contributing less wait 5 seconds. This method does r
work as well in a general discussion since it often becomes very
draggy, but trying to be conscious of slowing down the pace of a
discussion can be helpful in providing people space to speak and
cutting down on interrupting.
3. Groups may want to use roleplays to examine the problems they are
having. Doing the roleplay first portraying the problem that exists, and the
re-running it one or more times incorporating possible solutions can be
helpful. However, it is essential that it not make an example of particular
people whose functioning in the group may be presenting problems.
Roleplays can also be a good way of practicing and sharpening new skills,
and of thinking about how to use group skills in other settings.

Resources:

Much of the written material on group process is academically oriented,
and is not pertinent to groups attempting to function in an egalitarian way,
incorporating both a work task and elements of personal growth and suppc
as macro-analysis seminars do. A manual which has a very useful section
group dynamics pertaining to this kind of group is the monster manual (se
listing under COMMUNITY BUILDING). A more traditional academic sourc
is DYNAMICS OF GROUPS AT WORK by Herbert Thelan (University of
Chicago Press, 1954. $2.45 paperback). The first half is a case study of a
group of people in group process training. The second half is an analysis o
issues of group dynamics with suggestions of what people can do to help.

C. PERSONAL GROWTH (RE-EVALUATION COUNSELING)

For people who are interested in pursuing personal growth in an organiz
manner and want to learn a specific tool for this purpose. We also feel that
this might be helpful to people who have a good informational grasp of the
"macro" picture, and perhaps some idea of action they need and want to ta
but who find that feelings of powerlessness, fear of taking action, and othe
such factors prevent them from actually *doing* it. Many of the underlying
assumptions and techniques of the macro-analysis process (e.g. exciteme
sharing, positives stated first during evaluation) are shared with re-evaluat
counseling, and our experience with each discipline continues to challenge
and enrich the other. Thus, we feel that re-evaluation counseling, in additic
to being a helpful tool for our own personal growth, has specific relevance
helping us take effective social action.

Description:

Re-evaluation counseling (also known as co-counseling) is a
non-professional, peer counseling technique based on the assumption tha
all human beings are naturally creative, intelligent, zestful, and loving, anc

that the only thing which prevents us from acting this way *all* the time is the accumulation of distressing experiences which have happened to us. Human beings are equipped with methods for healing these distresses (laughing and crying, for example) but our society blocks us from using these healing processes effectively (for example: "Big boys don't cry"). Re-evaluation counseling is essentially a tool for recovering these methods of healing our distresses, and thus for becoming the creative, zestful, loving people we should all be.

Classes for learning the techniques of re-evaluation counseling are available in many parts of the country. To find out about classes closest to you write *Present Time*, 719 2nd Avenue North, Seattle, Washington 98109 and ask for a copy of the latest issue. It will contain a list of contact people. Call the one closest to you to find out about classes in your area.

THE HUMAN SIDE OF HUMAN BEINGS: THE THEORY OF RE-EVALUATION COUNSELING, Harvey Jackins. (Rational Island Publishers, PO Box 2081, Main Office Station, Seattle, Washington 98111.)
THE HUMAN SITUATION, Harvey Jackins. (Available as above.)
 Note: These books are not available from bookstores but only from the publisher or re-evaluation counseling teachers.

If possible, we strongly suggest attending a class. It is necessary to actively participate in re-evaluation counseling to effectively understand it. Reading about it does not convey it adequately.

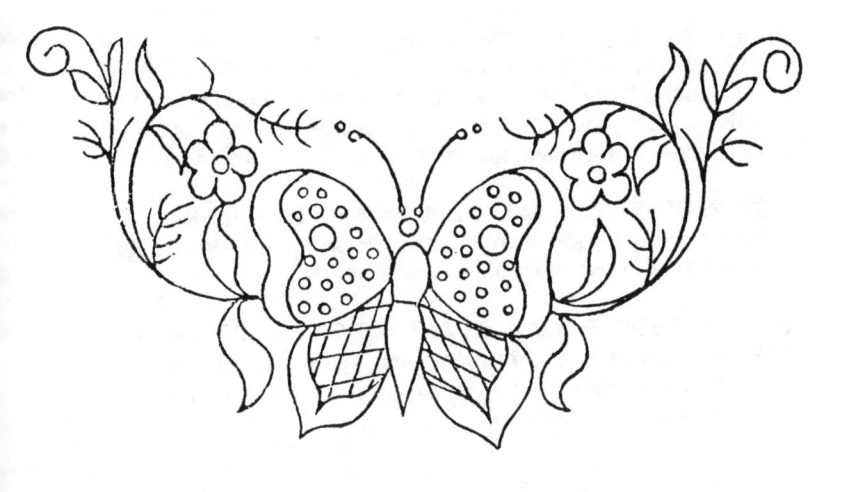

D. DIRECT ACTION

For a group that is ready to work together, or already is active, and knows what it wants to focus on, but lacks experience in doing direct action and needs more information and more confidence to take that step.

Ideas:
- Practice in small ways: a one-shot demonstration, leafletting, petition guerrilla theater, street-speaking.
- Role-play potential situations as preparation for doing them in real life
- Work up to bigger things (campaign against a nuclear plant, opposition to highway construction, etc.)

Resources: (*manuals*)

RESOURCE MANUAL FOR A LIVING REVOLUTION. See sections on preparation for action, action skills, how to build a good campaign, stages to non-violent social change; also the list at the end of groups and people around the country with knowledge and experience in this area.

A NONVIOLENT ACTION MANUAL, William Moyer. (Available from New Society Publishers for $1.75). A very practical nitty-gritty manual for campaigns and demonstrations.

THE POLITICS OF NONVIOLENT ACTION, Gene Sharp (Boston: Porter-Sargent, 1973. 3 vols. $2.95/$4.95/$5.95). An encyclopedia of tactics and strategies used throughout history. See especially Part II, "The Methods of Nonviolent Action," which examines in detail 198 specific methods of nonviolent action.

BLOCKADE! Richard K. Taylor. (Available from New Society Publishers, $3.95). The story of Movement for a New Society's successful blockade of secret U.S. arms shipments to Pakistan in 1971, which grew out of a macro-analysis seminar! Contains excellent nonviolent action manual.

HOW PEOPLE GET POWER, Si Kahn (McGraw-Hill, 1970). A handbook of effective organizational techniques and strategies for organizers to use in empowering people.

FOR THE PEOPLE: A CONSUMER ACTION HANDBOOK, Joanne Manning Anderson, (Addison-Wesley, 1977; $5.95). A how-to-do-it book for consumer action. Details on running a news conference to "break a story" and more!

The Citizen Involvement Training Project (219 Hills House North, Division of Continuing Education, Amherst, MA 01003) puts out a series of basic manuals for citizen groups; they are $6.00 each: PLAYING THEIR GAME OUR WAY: USING THE POLITICAL PROCESS TO MEET COMMUNITY NEEDS (1978) by Greg Speeter. PLANNING AND PROGRAM DEVELOPMENT (1978) by Duane Dale PLANNING AND PROGRAM DEVELOPMENT (1978) bu Duane Dale and Nancy Mitiguy. POWER: A REPOSSESSION MANUAL: ORGANIZING STRATEGIES FOR CITIZENS (1978) by Greg Speeter. WE INTERRUPT THIS PROGRAM...A CITIZEN'S GUIDE TO USING THE MEDIA FOR SOCIAL CHANGE (1978) by Robbie Gordon. THE RICH GET RICHER AND THE POOR WRITE PROPOSALS (1978) by Nancy Mitiguy.

PEOPLE POWER, U.S. Office of Consumer Afairs (1980-free!). An excellent 411-page encyclopedic guide, originally meant to demonstrate "What Communities are Doing to Counter Inflation." Again, though little or no political context, an extraordinarily useful manual for learning how to research abuses and think about alternatives in housing, food production and provision, community development, energy, transportation, and health.

E. HOW TO RESEARCH YOUR COMMUNITY

For groups with a good macro perspective who need to transfer that understanding to a local level in order to move forward in action—to begin speaking to immediate local issues from a macro perspective.

Ideas:
- Go door-to-door with questionnaires.
- Brainstorm issues you want more information on, assign different people to research them out.
- Check out the local experts—old timers, local activists, sympathetic councilpersons, information bureaus, people's yellow pages, etc.

Resources:

STUDYING YOUR COMMUNITY, Roland L. Warren (Free Press, 1955; $3.95) "An exhaustive aid for the organizer or journalist undertaking a total community study—including how to conduct a community survey and a smattering of example charts and maps. The bulk of the book is in chapters exploring a particular aspect of the community: housing, economic life, communications, religious activities, etc. References, to books and organizations, and up to 200 prying questions in each chapter, are leads to uncovering the functions of these institutions. Though devoid of any political context, it is without question the most comprehensive book in its field for lay people."

NACLA RESEARCH METHODOLOGY GUIDE (North American Congress on Latin America, 1970, $1.50). "Offering methods that range from 'back-room' investigations to the use of establishment sources and trade magazines, NACLA urges the study of elites, political parties, corporations, the media empire, labor, the university-military-industrial complex, police, church, the health industry and imperialism. We need to understand the structures we're fighting—a valuable tool."

OPEN THE BOOKS: HOW TO RESEARCH A CORPORATION, (Urban Planning Aid, 1974, $1.50). "A lively action-oriented guide that gives scores of information sources and tips on how to extract relevant facts. Discussions cover small and large corporations, subsidiaries, real estate companies, and multinationals... with a separate chapter on how to read financial statements. Introductions and examples give a strong political context and suggestions on how information can be used."

RESOURCES AVAILABLE FROM NEW SOCIETY PUBLISHERS
(all items postpaid; prices subject to change)

Moving Toward a New Society. Gowan, Lakey, Moyer & Taylor. Analysis, vision and strategy for a decentralized, democratic, and caring society. $6.00

Resource Manual for a Living Revolution, alias "the monster manual." Coover, Deacon, Esser, and Moore. Skills and resources for organizing for change from a nonviolent perspective. $8.95

Building Social Change Communties. Training/Action Affinity Group. "How-to-do-it" book for people looking to work with people to change the world. $4.95

A Manifesto for Nonviolent Revolution. Lakey. Original working draft outlining analysis, vision, and strategy for the MNS Network. $1.15

New Society Packet. The MNS statement of purpose; includes papers on analysis, visions, struggle, training, alternative institutions, community life-styles, and the network; and a bibliography. $1.15

Food and Hunger Macro-Analysis Seminar. Thorne & Moyer. $5.50

Blockade! Taylor. Story of MNS blockade of U.S. arms shipments to Pakistan. Includes a nonviolent action manual. $3.95

Taking Charge. Simple Living Collective. Step-by-step suggestions, from personal to political change. $3.25

Clearness: Processes for Supporting Individuals and Groups in Decision-Making. Woodrow. $2.25

Empowerment: Personal and Political Change. Pike. Essays, poems, and other "stuff" on the empowerment theme. $2.25

Leadership for Change. Kokopeli & Lakey. Looking at leadership and group functioning from a feminist perspective. $2.25

Manual for Group Facilitation. Center for Conflict Resolution. Excellent resource for group and workshop leaders and community builders. $5.50

Tell the American People: Perspectives on the Iranian Revolution. Albert, ed. Essays and photographs examining the processes of the Iranian Revolution, its hopes and problems. $5.95

Theory of Sexism. Bedard & Castle. $1.40
Working Toward a New Society and a Critique of American Marxism. Albert. $1.75
Organization and Strategy: Lessons from SDS, and Critique of a Mass Party Strategy. Irwin. $1.75
Off Their Backs and On Our Own Two Feet. Men Against Patriarchy. Men's writing on understand and overcoming sexism. $1.75
A Nonviolent Action Manual. Moyer. $1.75
Meeting Facilitation: The No-Magic Method. $.60
No More Plastic Jesus: Global Justice and Christian Lifestyle. Finnerty. $4.45
Why Nonviolence: Nonviolence Theory and Strategy for the Anti-Nuclear Movement. Irwin & Faison. 25¢
Energy for a New Society: Visions of a People's Energy Future. Albert, Faison, Finley & Moyer. 25¢
New Society Times & Changes: Lesbians, Gays Expose Abuse. 25¢

Make checks payable to: Movement for a New Society

To order literature, for a complete literature list, or for more information about MNS, contact:
 New Society Publishers
 4722 Baltimore Avenue
 Philadelphia, PA 19143

NEW SOCIETY PUBLISHERS is a collective of MOVEMENT FOR A NEW SOCIETY, a network of small groups working for fundamental social change through nonviolent action. Together we are developing an *analysis* of the present social order, a *vision* of a decentralized, democratic and caring society, a *strategy* for change through nonviolent action, and a *program* rooted in changed values and changed lives.